NEW YORK REVIEW BOOKS

POETS

NACHOEM M. WIJNBERG is the author u. ...
twenty poetry collections. His poetry has received many of the most
important Dutch and Belgian literary awards, including the 2018 P. C.
Hooft Award for lifetime achievement. His work has been widely
translated, with collections published in English, German, French,
Italian, and Afrikaans. Wijnberg is also an economist and a professor
at the University of Amsterdam Business School.

DAVID COLMER is a prolific translator of Dutch-language
literature. He translates from a range of genres and has won many prizes,
including the IMPAC Dublin Literary Award and the Independent
Foreign Fiction Prize (both with novelist Gerbrand Bakker). In 2021 he
was awarded the James Brockway Prize for his body of work as a poetry
translator. Recent translations include works by Radna Fabias and
Willem Frederik Hermans.

Nachoem M. Wijnberg

TRANSLATED FROM THE DUTCH
BY DAVID COLMER

NYRB/POETS

 NEW YORK REVIEW BOOKS   *New York*

THIS IS A NEW YORK REVIEW BOOK
PUBLISHED BY THE NEW YORK REVIEW OF BOOKS
435 Hudson Street, New York, NY 10014
www.nyrb.com

This publication has been made possible
with financial support from the
Dutch Foundation for Literature.

N ederlands
letterenfonds
dutch foundation
for literature

Library of Congress Cataloging-in-Publication Data
Names: Wijnberg, Nachoem M., 1961– author. | Colmer, David, 1960– translator.
Title: Nachoem M. Wijnberg / by Nachoem M. Wijnberg; translated by David Colmer
Description: New York: New York Review Books, [2022] | Series: New York review
  books poets
Identifiers: LCCN 2022000705 (print) | LCCN 2022000706 (ebook) | ISBN
  9781681376523 (paperback) | ISBN 9781681376530 (ebook)
Subjects: LCSH: Wijnberg, Nachoem M., 1961—Translations into English. | LCGFT:
  Poetry.

ISBN 978-1-68137-652-3
Available as an electronic book; ISBN 978-1-68137-653-0

Cover and book design by Emily Singer

Printed in the United States of America on acid-free paper.
10 9 8 7 6 5 4 3 2 1

Contents

from **SLOW AND GENTLE (1993)**

from **IS THIS BETTER (1994)**

from **JEWISH POEMS (2020)**

from **NAMING NAMES (2022)**

Hotel to Airport

Promise the taxi driver:
half as much again
without the radio
(and all the windows open).
They built the city
on a hillside;
when the taxi reaches the bottom
the moon is next to the city.

The driver keeps
his side of the deal:
no sound except
his Chrysler, no moon
other than left of the city.

Bernard Berenson Writes to His Sister

Every morning I stroll through the Louvre
and in the evening I watch Sarah Bernhardt's hands.
I do not waste my time, I fill myself with beauty
in all its forms—I have an insatiable hunger for beauty—
I have also become more intelligent. If the people
of Boston
ask what I am planning upon my return,
do not answer them. I am learning so much here.
Compared to Paris, their Harvard will always remain
a kindergarten—send me seventy-five dollars

or a hundred dollars. Borrow it
from the good people of Boston.
If they think I am riding a gray horse back and forth
in the Bois de Boulogne—let them think so!—
I rub my face raw on beauty. I do not waste my time.

Caesar Visits Cicero

He sits across from me.
He arranges his hair
with just one finger.
Behind him evening falls.
We are sitting at a table surrounded by trees.
He moves a slender hand through the air.
He behaves in a way that makes the people love him.
Soldiers who have never shown any aptitude
are suddenly prepared to do anything
to the greater glory of Caesar.
Overthrowing the state
is something inconceivable
for good men.
Soldiers die for him
differently than they would die for the state.
I tell him,
overthrowing the state
is something I cannot support.
I too am prepared to die for the state.
Behind him it is evening.
I tell him I love him.
He extends his hand toward me
and holds his hand in the air.

Instructions for Regimental Officers

It is important to explain to your new wife
the mechanism of the lunar eclipse
as soon as possible after the honeymoon.
This way she will not be afraid
if one occurs and she remembers
what other women have probably told her.
One night you can ride in a circle (try not
to make it an ellipse) between two trees while
shouting the explanation a number of times.

If she is young enough she will believe you
as you ride through the darkness in a circle.

Achilles

The hero Achilles. On a chair
with armrests. With a thinking
expression. His weapons
standing upright behind him.

He has laid them aside. The points
that have brought death stabbed
into the sand. The kings say:
enough.

A group of noisy kings
praise his looks. With the priests
they slaughter animals.

Without him. He sits in a chair
with armrests. He burns
his part of the city.

Second Man

If a man has traveled on a train
with a second man and that
second man dies, the other
accepts the rest of his life.

He gets off the train after it has
arrived and walks through the cold
night air with his coat hanging open
to the forbidden far side of the station.

There, he looks at the tracks
and the lights and a detached engine
parked on the tracks.

Large and dark. A man who
traveled together with another man,
who died, owes him this.

Analysis and Organization

Completely empty space
is unimaginable and immeasurable.
A bird is organized so that it is unnecessary
to assume an immeasurable substance
inside its body that remains after its death.
Coleridge walked extremely slowly and spoke as if drunk
of a hundred subjects before saying goodbye.
He hoped that the influences of philosophy and poetry
would not cancel each other out, leaving nothing.

The identical is interchangeable.
It follows that the loss of the self on death only proves
that the self is not as it thinks it is and addresses
and seems immeasurable to itself.
Humphry Davy, who had isolated new substances
(which neither he nor others could break down further),
accompanied Coleridge on that morning walk.
Coleridge said that the birds would die out.

Qualities depend on the organization of components.
Coleridge remembered their conversation as lasting
approximately one minute but it was much longer,
and the empty sky extended constantly.

The Writers

Leo Tolstoy on Anton Chekhov:
if he weren't a doctor he would write even better.
And also: he doesn't believe in God.
And also: enormously talented but his starting point
is materialistic, conceited, and wrong.

In each year of Chekhov's life he built
a house, a bridge, a school.
He said: like an Arab who at least plants a tree
or digs a well in his lifetime.
And he planted rows of trees in his garden
and when his body grew weaker he had a chair
put down on the earth and sat in it in a dressing gown
while a man planted a tree according to his instructions
and he decided that the tree also counted for that man
and only paid him for carrying the chair to the tree.

In the winter of 1942 Stalin ordered
the giant Tolstoy exhumed and brought back to life.
He stood three meters tall barefoot in the snow
and snatched incoming German aircraft out of the sky,
listening to Stalin's whispered explanation.

Anton Chekhov on Leo Tolstoy:
as long as he exists, one can call oneself a writer;
even if one doesn't produce anything oneself, his work
is sufficient justification for all our efforts and hope.

Alaska

With the wind behind him a man walks over the ice
until he is exhausted and only then turns back.
He built the bed in which his last friend
and a woman lay awake, motionless and naked
           the morning after their wedding.
When a man died, even an unimportant man,
he could take away all the shadow falling on him
by asking his friends to step back.

He sieved the river water that contained gold
through his fingers and had a photograph of himself
           taken standing on the bank
together with his friends and an unknown woman,
in the new suits he had bought with the gold.
His friends would have thrown themselves at the walls
if he was dying in a house, without waiting
           for his question.

Slowly it pushes the pile of snow
it is hiding behind over the glittering ice
toward a man who is blind to this change,
although just above it birds
are flying with it into the wind,
and only disperse at the last moment,
when the bear leaps and glides like one of them.

The Noise in Rodin's Studio

His students only ever make hands
and put them on the shelves, arranged by category.
He himself shapes the bodies from clay
and attaches the prepared hands to them.
He folds out openings, moistening the clay
with spit from his mouth to save time.
He walks between the piles of clay and the models
kneeling on sheets while the students watch,
holding hands that grasp and release.

Plan

Her body is a commentary on bodies,
clarifying what is possible and what is meaningful.
She wants to be carried or learn to move
as if steering her body with her hands and her feet.
Her skin is softer than paper or water
and her body has more time if it makes its choices
as if working on the solution of an important problem.
She has a plan: get furious on the street
and let a passerby calm her down.
She wants to feel like a fourteen-year-old
and feel the weight of a man on her while he refuses
to enjoy her before she is old enough
and stands up to ask for postponement for both of them.

The Destination

The princess traveled as a gift
to the north and took silk with her
so she could be well dressed beside the man
who had been appeased with her.
Past the border, riders awaited her,
arranged like words in an incomprehensible poem,
or stars that, distributed seemingly at random,
determine the outcome of lives.

The Horse

A righteous man arrived on horseback.
He slept with all the women of the village
without paying attention to hands or faces.
The horse stood over him when he lay
with a woman in a field. When he disappeared
into a house, the horse waited at the entrance.

When people saw the horse by itself they threw
sharp stones and sand at it. They took away
the feed the man had put out for the horse.
The horse's skin was torn and the horse grew
thinner and thinner. Finally the horse could no
longer stand up with the man in the saddle.

From then on they walked alongside each other
through the village. Even the younger women
imitated the horse's whinnying and frightened glances.

Birthdays

Sometimes river islands, sometimes oceanic islands.
The world has six great rulers:
the ruler of Morocco, of Egypt, of India,
of China, the two Khans of Asia.
The persons he was a year ago,
two years ago, and so on, join him
to whisper good luck in the ear of the person he will be,
just as he was whispered to when he awoke.
He grows rich from tokens of hospitality,
though bandits sometimes rob him of all he has.
Diseases pursue him or catch up to him
and leave him behind.
Despite his incomplete knowledge of the law
he was appointed a judge in Madagascar,
in Anatolia, in India.
He introduces new holidays on warm blue islands.
Towers have been raised on the coasts of those islands
to watch for his return so it can be celebrated.

Mountains

Fortunately he has some understanding of landscape
and this reduces his loneliness
as he treks through the mountains like what's left
of an army that defended a pass against a superior force
     or the first of that army to arrive.

Travelers look at waterfalls
and rest from the journey to them.
A woman washes her long hair in the vertical water,
     a man his hands,
and together they search for the hut of a hermit
     who is not at home.

Assignments

A man walks into a café,
asks for a coffee, puts so much sugar in it
that the cup overflows, drinks the coffee, asks the woman
at the counter for a light for a cigarette he's already put
                                in his mouth, is given a light, pays.
A man walks into a restaurant
that is being cleaned early one morning
and asks the first person to look in his direction
for a hot meal and where he can sit down to rest.
A man suffers something like the death of an only child,
something that makes his life different
from how he had imagined it up to then,
and tells people who hadn't intended to get to know him
                                about it.
A man is left behind in a forest with two kinds of trees
and at the bottom of some of the hills
there are treeless areas with swings and slides
and merry-go-rounds he has to push himself.
A man is brought into possession of a story about his life
up to the moment something terrible happens to him
and it is left to him to make use of it or not.

Letter to the Corinthians

Beginning: primitive society.
Everyone negotiates blindfold about who
will be a hunter and who a fisher, without involving
fish or foxes because they cannot think about
their own thoughts. Their eyes stay open.
Awareness of the world as well as ourselves
is as difficult for us as self-awareness for fish or foxes
although they in their behavior take their own existence
into account as we do the existence of the world.
Faith as a substitute for awareness of the world,
which for superman has the same nature as his cogito.

Continuation: political society.
Love as protection and touch and, together with faith,
remedy for the fear of incomprehension and inattentiveness.
Hope as hope for understanding and sufficient information
to be able to make choices without faith or love
and to choose roles; commanding, obeying,
or even the role of those who are ruled by love
and therefore not responsible
and incomprehensible to themselves.

Conclusion: night.
Does anyone think it's a good idea to fall in love
                            with superman?
Let them blindfold a fish or a fox and negotiate with it.

End of the Night

Some stand at the sea as if in a bar,
some as in a crowded bar where they cannot move
without pushing others out of the way,
some as in an empty bar,
some as at the start of night, some as at the end of night,
when more light is being made to announce the sun.

Some follow someone else cycling ahead of them
to visit a house in which staircases spiral
until the points of the compass disappear
                        like the dimmest stars.
Some wait in a sitting room and lie on a couch
and flip through a text book, a cook book,
                        the Yellow Pages.
Some wait in a bedroom, immediately under the roof,
and look at the pattern of the quilt cover, the rafters,
the green light of an electric clock. For some,
music is turned on while they wait. Some
are sniffed by two dogs, one older and more loved.

Some are led to a house in a sea of gravel
with a garden behind it
with fruit trees and shrubs and grass.
A stack of telephone books behind a couch
in the sitting room, closed ranks of pot plants
                        on wide windowsills,
the lowest windows transparent,
the top ones colored glass,
a small bronze statue of a man with rubber bands
                        around his neck and arms.
In the attic: a double bed with broken chairs on it,
a large grinding wheel for sharpening knives, a mirror,
kitchen scales, dark dried-out apples.
In the garage: a car, rope, a four-pronged rake.

Night goes on lightly. No one blesses anyone.

The List of Foreigners

In the daytime wild animals walk across the beach
and we stay in the hotel or its immediate surroundings.
We were invited to take part in conversations
to become familiar with at least one other person.
The maids on nightshift take off their work clothes
when they go into the ocean, facing the first sun.
They all turn their heads away at the same time
                        when a wave hits them.
In the bus home they fan themselves with their blouses
and at home they make hot and filling breakfasts
for their children before going to bed.

The houses close to the beach have swimming pools.
In this way the city blends without a clear border
into the ocean and there are ships with sailors.
Events take place in rooms intended for that purpose,
behind glass and in light: exercising muscles,
                         unwrapping gifts.
A man walking through a shopping street on a Sunday
has five fantasies he can carry out in the clothes
                he is wearing.
The sky clears every morning with great rapidity
and cobwebs of light appear in the swimming pools
and on skin that is covered with water.

After breakfast we walk through the reception hall
or through the streets immediately surrounding the hotel.
Requests that must always be answered:
the way, the time.

Farce

Every time she sees the husband she faints.
The husband invariably fells the lover
                              with a single blow.
At night the sleepless husband sits at a table
wearing striped pajamas and with
an almost empty cognac glass in front of him.
She meets the lover on rough grass at the foot of a hill,
close to a neglected zoo; monkeys surrounded by feces
and empty ice-cream containers, bears with dusty coats,
deer and wild horses lying on their sides
                              and breathing heavily.

Saying Goodbye to a Friend

Saying goodbye to a friend who is traveling far
to where he has no friends.
We say goodbye in the hills outside of town
and I watch him until he disappears out of sight,
forcing myself not to shout more words
that will remind him of a good hour of our friendship.
I walk home as empty as clothes,
unable to expect a guest like that traveler.

Summer Storm

Every year he can lose as much as this year
without becoming desperate or needing to ask his
                creditors for forgiveness.
Behind him, wooded hills and a river with swans.
Dark curly hair, light eyes, all skin blemishes visible
    in the light before a thunderstorm.

Solitary and subsiding houses on hills,
abandoned walls, trees with green leaves
                glittering and heavy from the rain,
lightning-split trees, a landing wharf with water
    washing over it, small ships at anchor.
Every year he can lose as much as this year.

The Expedition to Cathay

The queen who is married to a cheat
and has married her daughters off
to two other cheats gives him three ships
and a letter to the king of earthly paradise
so he will return to her with a reply.

Branches and leaves are carried on the waves
and their greenness proves that land cannot be far;
as does the number of birds flying in a certain direction
and the temperature of the water. Furred animals emerge
from cold water but to warm water come lions.

Tall trees stand so close together that on some islands
no sunlight reaches the ground and the birds
have so many colors they are like remnants of a world
that has burst apart. A naked king offers to sail back
with him, accompanied by his daughters,
                                    as further proof.

This ocean is like a lake and only meals
and prayers interrupt the cloudless days.
A group of women could steer the ship—
drowsy, drinking sweet wine, their heavy skirts
catching what's left of the wind while they
                        stroll the deck as if in a park.

The sailors rest below, surrounded by naked bodies.
When the sun sets, the admiral sees from the shape
                        and direction
of the last shadow on deck that the course is perfect
and the ship is propelled along the degree of latitude
of Jerusalem as by a gigantic, sure hand.

The abandoned ship drifts to the coast. Strong winds
and waves that suddenly rise in the water
steer the ship and make it pick up speed.
The stone king and queen are upright in the water,
not lying on their backs, not kneeling beside each other.

He stands behind her chair. His cloak and her dress
are draped over the pedestal but their folds do not touch.
Her right hand grasps the arm of the chair. Perhaps
they shouted all their servants awake in the night
and had their servants place them on the edge
                                of the splashing water.

Boxer

His mother is fast but his father slow,
and he too becomes slow.

His father no longer gets up out of his chair
before it grows dark.

His mother picks him up from school in a taxi
and tells him to get a job.

He becomes the slowest boxer;
always plenty of time for his opponent.

He fights boxers nobody ever thought
capable of winning again.

In a bar a man challenges him to a fight
and turns out to be a boxer
and injures him for months.

Brothel on the Beach

The gentlemen appear on the terrace,
descend the stairs,
walk to the ocean in their suits,
brothel white,
squat on the beach under their hats,
brothel white, wet with sweat.

The gentlemen take off their shoes,
brothel white,
and step into the water of the ocean,
warmer than their feet,
and look at the distant lightning,
cutting through the night, above the ocean.

The gentlemen run in a line
through the rain,
they do knee bends, and the ladies lie
between white sheets,
grains of sand in their hair, as beautiful as spies,
but softer, even than one who is sad.

When the rain and the night have passed
the ladies appear
in white nightgowns, with twirling parasols
in their hands,
and wash themselves with sponges and ocean water,
comb each other's hair, praise each other's breasts.

When the sun is high they lie on towels,
as on dark cushions
in jewelry stores, too tired to speak,
too hot to sleep,
sometimes digging beside the towel with one hand
and not finding anything, tearing their nails.

I Am a Doctor

I let rain destroy my clothes
and stay up all night and fall asleep
on the backseat of my car, on my horse.
If I find a dead body on the street
I search the pockets for letters and keys
and try to find someone who recognizes the body
(sometimes it is the dog or the horse).

Look at me, I am a doctor.
Give me your hand, I am a doctor.
Let me through, I am a doctor, no, a cop.
No, a doctor and a cop were walking down the road.

Here are two envelopes.
One contains a joke that is twice as good as the joke
                                in the other.
You can keep one of the two jokes.
Choose an envelope, open it, read the joke.
The joke in the other envelope is twice or half as good.
If I let you swap, would you?

What's it about, I asked everyone I found,
and they all told me the same joke about themselves
and they also gave me lists of their traits
as if they wanted to be in a better one.
It's me, talk to me.

I am a doctor, people called me to be sure.

I'm going to make a joke that will stay good
                        for ten years.
I have all the ingredients.

Freighter

The red freighter is moored at the wharf
in dark water: don't smoke!
But it is evening, it is evening,
and the people out walking are smoking on the wharf.

Their days are finished and they buy
cans of beer and roast potatoes,
and stare at the red freighter
at the wharf, squeezed between two cranes.

The red freighter in the dark water
that is still and dirty,
and the people smoking on the wharf,
and the ship whispers: don't smoke, as if for their lungs.

They drink from bottles they've brought with them
feel breasts for lungs,
with eyes closed they listen to the breathing
and shout: don't sink!

Bread

Enlarge your name by entering a small village
in the mountains
where a wedding is being celebrated.
There is no child that hasn't harmed its parents,
I will be a good mother,
these beads, this embroidery were made by my mother.

A laughing dark-eyed girl
holding a condom up to a restroom mirror.
Ponder this image as a memory for a funeral speech.
She beckons with one finger, blows a kiss.

Life is a party
and the heart is a sponge,
an inwardly branching series of hollows and filling,
hollows in filling and floating splinters of filling in hollows.

Breasts and buttocks of white bread
in threadbare underwear,
but in soft light she is soft
and the lament she sings is pure.

Dog

A dog has had enough
because it has felt poorly all week.

It says: I don't believe this is going to change
and I can't bear it anymore;
I feel so sorry for myself I can hardly breathe.

I no longer hear my voice except through my jawbone.
I will go outside with you
and then hope you no longer call my name.

Method

He touches up dead animals with colored ink
and eats peas before counting them.
He makes numbers with dice.
The twins he compares exist only in his mind.
Walking on the beach he gets an idea
and immediately guesses its incorrectness.
He draws glasses and mustaches on photos
and vaginas on bald heads and writes: two weeks later.
He feeds mice and rabbits without putting gloves on first
and whispers to them of his hope.

Dance Music

I take away the difference between pieces with
                              and without excitement.
Before changing music you'd better learn how to fight
because you will have to defend yourself on the street,
in the dark between two broken streetlights,
alone against the many who have noticed that you have
                              changed their dance music.
I take away the difference between before
                              and after menace.
I make footsteps in the dark in a street
                    that is growing longer.
You'd best learn to protect your fingers in an iron glove
like a long glove on a woman who has learnt how
                              to undress to music.
They hear repetitions and only notice days later that
                    they were not, not repetitions,
and screaming they run out into the street to search
                                        for me
and screaming they run out into the street to search
                                        for me
as they notice I have made farewell music they can't
                    dance to. Goodbye, night!

Long Bright Night

Don't look at yourself, or rather,
don't look at yourself for more than ten minutes.
But you can take a photo in those ten minutes
then lay the camera aside and fall asleep with yourself
so that you have a photo of your body
when it was for you, and ten minutes remains
                              the maximum
for looking at yourself as if you have paid for it.

The bright night is a sorting machine
with vibrating drums, conveyor belts, paddle wheels,
suction magnets, the desire to go away as far as possible,
and what is left has a uniform size and melting point.

Maybe everything you do will then become
                              important to you
and you will start paying attention to your hand speed
like a pianist or a prize fighter or your trainer
                              or your servant.

You want to stiffen while swinging something
and while taking a long step, almost a leap.
Give me something to eat and I will shape and cut it,
into a hippopotamus for instance.
I want to work in stone but no one gives me a stone.

You are too tired for easy things
and too tired for difficult things
and you are too tired for easy things, you look away.
My hands are broken, my mouth is torn, but not really.
Give me something that is hard but not too hard for me.

Debate

I have already provided
so many arguments
without inconsistencies.
I am tired and want to stop.

What else can I appeal to:
a dream I had,
a newspaper report,
one of Rashi's opinions?

The scholars of the Rhineland were killed,
there were no more scholars in Mainz and Worms,
in Troyes there was Rashi.
No sentence can escape its literal meaning.

By way of comparison, suppose:
all schools have been burnt down
and a man who broke off his studies to support
                                        his family
writes down what he has learnt and what he could
                                        have learnt.

What else can I appeal to:
one of Rashi's doubts,
the tears in my eyes when I think of the start of his work,
my weariness?

I want to wash and eat
and read a book
that I found magnificent when I first read it
and have partly forgotten.

A book in which each sentence
has at least a literal meaning,
which can be forgotten
and rediscovered unspoilt.

Perhaps my rights have been exhausted
but then too I ask
to be allowed to stop
and rest my head on my arms.

Free Day

A judge says: rules of conduct help
as much as beautiful music, in the best case,
and in the way that contests and elections help.
So difficult to sympathize with more than one at once,
but a winner in the morning and a loser in the evening
is at least possible and maybe practice
with music that moves in two directions at once.

A judge says: I mustn't simplify
and nurse my lack of understanding
from when I first wake up
on a day of judgment and I don't listen to those
who present themselves as understandable
and bring forward however many witnesses to this.

A judge says: dignity is what can make me cry
when it comes about or breaks
or in a face that keeps suppressing its crying
or scream into the wind drunk with dignity.

A judge says: I can no longer remember an act
or assume hidden reasons for an act
or consider an act involuntary
—a stone, a part of an empty landscape—
or I cannot let the actor out of my thoughts for a second
but consider them my landscape
and my only guide out of it.

A judge says: music strengthens compassion,
at least as long as it lasts,
and contests and elections also help
and go with free days until no freed person
is concerned about the outcome and celebrates the day as
someone with unquestioned dignity.

As If in a Dark Palace

Could you stay longer tonight
or could you wish me a night
that is just like it
with what you say in the dark to someone
                              who cannot yet speak,
can no longer speak, does not want to speak?
As if from a palace about a desert
and a man in it with another man, deceitful and generous,
shaking his head, asking for no.

Weeks

Weeks and he doesn't appear in his dreams.
It can't go on like this.
How else? A game before breakfast
with prizes for everything like at a birthday party
and more prizes for those who skin their knees
or have to leave early?

Like His

Who is not a friend of a body
like his, with right-of-way?
In one brief day it can change,
and they try to chop off the hand with which
                    he points to himself,
catching up to him when he flees.
He is most grateful.

Report

A hospitable man's house collapses,
crushing everyone except one person who runs away
and tells a man who gives his wife
and what he owns to the messenger and runs away.
Some messengers are out of breath and cannot yet speak,
but the messenger who told me I was a rich
and hospitable man smelled of fasting,
had grayish skin, scratched himself while speaking.

How It Was Surprising

On the stairs she pulls him toward her
and asks him to touch her everywhere, not wait.
How it was surprising that it was possible
when others were present.
With that in mind he tries to recover
what he thought was possible, being one of those they said
                              he no longer belonged with.
At first he thought they had told him that
by tearing the clothes he was wearing when others were
                                                    present.

Naked

They lead me to a bathtub filled with hot water.
Lying next to the bath are clothes for me to put on.
At dinner they give me wine
and the best cuts of meat, and when I stop eating
they ask me who I am, and what has brought me here.
After I have answered, the host leads me to a bed.
He lies down on his bed and his wife comes to lie beside him
and she talks to him about what to give me when I go.

Grass

A boy walks up to me and says:
there is a beautiful woman in the next village.
I only need to follow him.
She does not remind you of anything, she prepares.
On the roadside grass two large and hairy men are wrestling.
The boy says he checked the grass for them.
They are her brothers, they don't like being watched.
In exchange they gave him this receiving.

The Way You Like to See Me

There was mist in the dark
and I said goodbye and goodbye
and was calm on the train,
my eyes at the cold window.

Movement

He gets the animals moving
by walking toward them while reaching out to them
and drives them toward the ravine hidden
by the tall grass and the gentle slope.
One day he dug a hole in the ground to sleep
and nothing in it was unusual,
gleaming white bones, teeth like grass,
to swap for weeks for what he wanted or suddenly
                                    give away.

Must You Always Be Reminded of This

What do you need to think up in advance?
Do you have to pay attention to what happens
                                    after something else,
only to be surprised when it doesn't,
like being allowed to eat something that was slaughtered
                                    without you in mind?
Wouldn't it be better to put each part back
where you remember it coming from,
not thinking if something is more urgent
or what you want to think about afterwards,
and washing your hands and face when you are finished,
without hurrying, so you don't have to do it over again?
Must you follow the detailed instructions
                                    you once thought up,
and learnt by heart, destroying the notes?

If There Is Salvation Outside the Law

Who with whom in a conservation law?

The bodies do not need to be differentiated,
not by me; let them do that themselves,
if they want to live,
           like the sun and the sea.

The law honors bodies,
does not like them just disappearing.

One to slaughter and burn,
one to send into the wilderness,
so you can be pointed in the right direction
by someone who is headed that way anyway:
go now.

It Has Been Going On for a Long Time

Sunrise is over.
That's what it's like with something I know by heart.

Help me to feel happy,

so I can say: it has been going on for so long now,
I can't stop anymore.

So slow in this landscape

where a single glance is enough
for gods and gigantic goddesses.

Slower than a life goes by.

Ever see a horse running before it's fully light?
My eyes linger on it but how could it be enough
along the lines of: if only I were freed from my
                            imprisonment,
it would be enough,

and hadn't been given anything else, it would be enough.

If the earth sets,
let it set behind a head like the sun.

Someone said to me: I want to hear you
try to sing; that was when I stopped.

Out of Reach of My Hands

I heard that you wouldn't be mine much longer.
A light woman, in the air,
              not easy to approach.

Of course it's serious and you don't like it
when I imitate you:
              high kicks, split leaps,
which fail of course,

        without the required body
of light and air.

No show for me, practice required.
Do not imitate!
              Doing a somersault
with a cigar in my mouth, the nonsense that drives me.

              What kind of sight is that?

              What kind of air is it,
what expectation does it raise?

In what kind of light is it?
How many hands, the body

not mine much longer?

Psalm 22

Listen.
The words I cry out

like

a herd,
trampling the field,
and there is no other field.

A horse is drowning at the bottom of the waterfall,
my face is half covered with blood.

Does listening to me not distract you
from your sure and ongoing loss?

But I keep an eye open for you
so you can look through it
and look again and come up with an answer
and want to retract it again like an unintended but
                                    released offering.

Like saying: I do not want
to lose you.

Nice Work If You Can Get It

Her breasts thrusting forward in the sun
and the wind and the rain. In what not?

Maximum points for effort.

What she likes to hear:
standing next to you is like being
a vase in a corner behind a front door,
filled with a dozen wet umbrellas.

I used to think differently about how
to appeal to the most beautiful hearts:
never leave me, otherwise I'll cry
and smash chairs.

She kisses me on the cheek and asks me
to slap her loudly on the buttocks. She says:
don't do anything until you hear from me.

And I, the listener, unpracticed at dancing,

move my body like a tree
in the wind.

If I Still Have Rhythms

If I still have rhythms
I can take words out
and put them back again

they rob me of everything and stay with me,

in search of words that work
like shouted names
that do not travel from line
to line, not getting lost anywhere,

finally disappearing all alone, shattering,
and shouting doesn't help,

I can either stare at
rhyming rise and fall

or make the same word rhyme with the same word

or cut the word
that rhymes with

but I have neither rhyme nor rhythm
and can't cut like that.

Not Wanting to See It

Proving by making it balance,

sacrificing what consents.
No rain for a long time, trees die in dry wind.

Sacrificing to make amends, understanding proof,
proving understanding,
                    and if amends cannot be made,
if what should not have happened has happened,
an inadmissible sacrifice
made and seen,

never return to the garden-enclosed proof,

the garden enclosed by walls of proof

        in which rain falls until the walls
overflow and collapse.

It's Still Yours Even If I Now Take It Back

I remember a time I was running on the beach.
I ran to and fro and the footprints in the sand
were all mine.
I kept running; I didn't get tired.

A good table, far from Siberia.

I am very good at appropriating the memories
of others, to notice later that they had always,
as an undressed person says to their undresser,
always been yours.

I open a bottle of champagne, a better bottle this time,
and apologize again.

Yet another man who is scared for his memories
grabs me by the arm.
What do I want with the memories of a stranger
who can't go on without them?

What good are those beautiful memories to him now;
they're not worth anything anymore!
                    He says,
if he could, he would put them out with the garbage.

This ends with them entering dressed as memories,
bowing left and right.
        A farewell performance
and the proceeds are theirs alone.

Come see, aren't they sweet?

It's not the first champagne I've ever drunk,
glass-holding arms entangled so I no longer knew
from which glass.

With which intention?
To make which recovery more difficult?

    An old photograph
of a crowded street I used to walk down,
look if I happen to be in it,

if my face is looking just past me. Look,
that was me, your knowing what's happened to me since
makes you look at this photo for a long time.

Using time to stand in line

and looking back through the line
as if the openings for the eyes always stay in the same place
and the bodies can be twisted and stretched
until all the openings line up,

but there is no convincing beginning like a convincing end
like: but I spoke to him just yesterday.

Look, like a photo, and my face
is no longer in it.

I bought a box of chocolates,
the first thing I bought in a store,

and paid with coins I had picked up off the street.
On the way home I dropped the box
and those I gave it to didn't mention the broken chocolates.

I wanted shoes I had seen.
Those who gave me money found them too expensive
                                at first.
Boarding the bus home I forgot the box
and when I went back to the bus stop it was gone.

I was immediately given money for new ones.

I received a gift.
It was exactly what I wanted.
I would tell everything I could tell
about whatever I was asked.

If I had more of them I could open
a gift shop
and if I knew someone who would be willing to wait
in the shop all day for a customer like me

while outside light and heat make sick children
cry out in pain,

the lawns in the gardens are dried out but watering them now
would make them get scorched.

Another gift I forget to give myself,
not even having decided that I should be able to get by
without.

How does the skin feel today,
like astonishing nakedness?

We know each other so well it doesn't matter.

You didn't need to ask,
it has always been yours.

Guests Come, Guests Go

When someone who is blind
can suddenly see
they still walk like someone who is blind,
scared of forgetting how.

When someone who is blind
is suddenly no longer scared
of forgetting how,

of losing,
of seeing, not seeing,

of not being scared,
of saying goodbye
to the guests who didn't come.

The Poem of the Gifts

Thank-you list in the form of a wish list.
Wish list in the form of a thank-you list.
For the form of time,
for the reversibilities and orders of things.

For her with the enormous swinging hips,
at great distance like a metronome,
close by almost still at last,

after half an hour a hand movement.

Thanks for that, and for not using her eyes
at first, and then adding them afterwards.

Thanks for the order,
which feels good, I can say that, it is the meaning
that imposes itself on me, like darkness
when I wake in the dark.

I am glad to see her
and I run to see her.

Another woman might have wounded me with her eyes
and then turned away.

Or yet another, surprised while bathing,
might have taken her breasts in her hands
without looking at me.

For the dress she holds above her head
in her outstretched arms.

Lying naked she turns her back to me.
In the dark I see the shining white line of her waist
and raised thigh.

This happens at night.

Her black dress on a stick.

The first to touch the dress
can lead her away.

Thanks for being allowed to take home
the silence in which I can listen
to find out where to look
in the dark,

to feel for what appears beside me.

One floats on my left and the other on my right
and I try to touch both at once
because I think they will only want to come with me together

Or let me go with them, to where one lives
and the other as her guest,

where I drink water from a glass,
sit on the floor and keep my distance.

Do we look different to you now?

Practicing lying still,
with my eye in my mouth

after doing what I can
for all who are here.

The darkness descends
and I do not say: I am here.

Duns Scotus says that the relationship
between thought and being
is analogous to that between the world and God.

Augustine says that the light that lets him find his way
in the depths of his self is different.

Without self no language, without language no self,
without the existence of open categories;
for which thanks.

For the silence, a different one for each language,
and for the darkness that is real darkness.

In the depths of the black night, says John of the Cross,
where he is underwater, swallowed, swallowed.

This is how happy dictionaries fill themselves.

Hold Your Breath

To find out now
if the charts are right

if it is possible
to live
in monotonous desire,

looking at waves,
looking at coastlines
and at the charts,
following the finger on the chart,

floundering on the coagulated sea.

Returning now.
Not a single ship approaching
but a horizon-filling fleet sailing toward the open coast.

The participants, the investors, no longer need to be afraid,
those afraid for what might be missing from the fleet

no longer need to be afraid,

can rest in moving time
instead of clutching fear in their fists
like an amulet.

They find a piece of olive wood
on the beach that seems to contain a face,

take it to the man who frees the limbs
of statues, legs separating
as if walking, hands and arms stretching out,
eyes opening in sockets.

He is just tying the statues
of desire to chairs.

Is this the face of justice,
who does not need to justify her actions,
not even with further actions?

Who also no longer needs to be washed with water,
the eyes and lips moistened.

Now thought that is neither preparation nor judgment,
but disentangles,
arranges.

Forgiveness against irreparability,
against uncertainty, promises
of forgiveness.

A receding sea.

There

I am going there
where I am not expected.

Poorly tended trees
stand there.

If I had said but the slightest thing
I would have been expected.
Laughing loudly
until the trees fall,
roots twisting up out of the sandy soil.

Behind me, a wall or the sky.
No retort possible.

Right hand up, left hand, one or the other,

open hand, closed hand.

Active, moving, touching,
or at the other's mercy.
                Waves of.

Each time I think about it, I feel the same.

Burnt tree,
        standing black.
Always remember.

Two things I worry about:
the list that does not include sleep,
and that which I, if I leave now,

cannot do,
and I don't know if I still want to learn how.

A bird nailed to the ceiling.

Somewhere there stands a tree.

Where do I take, when the sea

no longer hugs the land with its waves,
no longer throws the castaway onto the beach
and awaits him in his new ship
among his hesitantly singing crew,

each holding his single wing,

where do I take, where do I put

my tree, where do I attach

my bird?

Still in my mind I am
            someone with few suitcases,
like someone looking for a successor among the quickest
            and most serious
pupils in the schools of many towns,

even if I am waiting like an extraordinary pupil,
            suitcases packed,
for the sign to leave everything behind.

Why not trees,
waves,
a big tree, the on-off switch for everything I see?

Saying that

instead of offering trees,
waves.

Look Left, Look Right

Under this sky I can't get elated
or dejected. Too calm, too clear; I can see further
than I reach. The guardians of darkness
dissolved, were slaughtered where they stood.

Dedicated to the Hours in Front of the Mirror

Starting everywhere and leading everywhere.
Day becomes night,
heavy makeup becomes light makeup, New Year's Eve
    becomes New Year's Day,

in the middle of the year like my bed moving in the middle.

Leading everywhere like an overdressed priest.

I Can Also Wish Them Something I Know Nobody Gets Anyway

Today I acted once again as if I can't do anything else
on this day, which is probably the most beautiful day of the
                                                        year.
I stood quietly at the door and listened before interrupting
                                                        you.
Let me tell you how outside clouds full of light are drifting
over the treetops.

His Name Is Lucky, They Ask Him to Carry Out the Proposal

Defending the proposal in a way that shows clearly
what it is: a mistake beyond regret, but they remain deaf
to crying out of fear of no longer crying
while mouth and eyes still can.

The Monologue About Power and Justice

Afterwards we will be compensated for everything
and compensated and beaming with joy and beauty
we will look in all directions with retrospectively
contrived pity—heart there, us here, so what.

Foreigner

The foreigner says: you were foreigners yourself once too,
and they say: no, not us, we've always been here,
waiting in the barren darkness for the body to be carried in
of someone who had always been here and met a foreigner.

The End of the Waiting

A light in the night,
answer to
another light,
answer to

another light
that says: someone
has come back to a palace
in which a woman

lies next to someone
like tired next to tired;
in another palace
lies softness that does not

flee from fingers
but allows fingers and says:
in me as in air
and no death for death.

Not Like a Bird

In women there are
smaller women,
sometimes larger women
and even larger women in those women.

The men
show those who cannot
by acting like they can only just:
sitting quietly in the shadows.

They show those who can fly,
not like a bird
but like a bird that has been taken
out of a bird and put back again.

At the Seaside

The girl walks to the sea
and at the seaside a man
asks: are you the girl
I was looking for?

She shakes her head,
holds out an open hand
on which he puts a ring
she will never lose for long.

He tells her how
she can recognize him
if she sees him again: he will
choose the other hand.

Be Sweet

He stands on one foot, then the other,
until he falls.
Unintentionally sitting on the ground,
he always laughs.

(Be sweet to me, just for a short while, not long.
May I postpone the short while?
Soon I will be kind to you, as you wish.
What do you want to do now?)

Sometime, one day, he will

(say: love me or leave me)

that is all I want.
Worrying deeply, pushing his hair
out of his eyes, because of whom, for whom?

On the Day of Atonement the girls of Jerusalem dance
in a field outside the city walls. The young men watch

and the girls call: one day you will have learnt
how to love me.
Promise me that you will wait
for that day and on that day wait for me.

Bird

A man starts to act like he is a bird,
waving his arms (if it doesn't work,
you know I'd be the first to admit it),
his wings' new walking companion.

Those who cannot walk gather round him,
cautiously appraising him,
along with devotees of clear machinery.
This is what a flying machine should look like!

Breath

Moon just above house, gray-blue clouds;
there was some red but it's gone.

Birds in trees and birds in the sky.

Gasping with desire. What is he in this desire?

Not being satisfied with
what he has been given; desiring what gets confused
before half-seen, with
a shorter season than desire.

Replying

Starting with what is the same for everyone

or can be (can everyone come over here),
looking at oneself and leaving out what reminds
one of oneself
to be able to say what can be said

without waiting until the same thing has been said in reply.

Understanding and loving, so that one of the two
can rest while the other watches.
Having the courage to say when no one is there:

how I had wanted to live is incomprehensible to me
but maybe not to everyone.

Remembering the start of seeing:
that wasn't me, that was someone else
who began to see
                            (I read or write
his life, or I love him).

I wished it was already over?

                        (Did I see in his life
how to recognize a love in hindsight?)

Horse and Bird

A horse and a bird agree
to help each other for a long time
while they change, becoming
more or less horse and bird.

A horse and a bird agree
to together watch the horse and bird
that help each other and not point out
where more help could be given.

Look up: not stars but birds
and on the ground horses that were born
with the smell of the sea in their nostrils
and compete with the birds.

(Someone would have preferred the horse
to disappear before the bird
to be able to speak with one
when the other was no longer there.)

Serious

They say if they are serious,
like people who have had something disappear forever,
or not serious,
letting themselves be wanted by whoever is closest,

now and over and over again,
when they are young and old.
Nobody says: that is not easy.
It is clear that they are not just saying it.

They take a bath,
dry themselves, say they will not do
what they said before.
Nobody says: they don't know what they want.

Bird Girl

Early in the morning
I met the bird girl.

Why are you so sad?
I asked her or she me.

Because the one who seeks me
comes when I am not here

and shouts and weeps
because I can't be found;

I can't hear it
and it makes me sad.

Laid down
the girl stands up
(let me stand up first,
I know the way).

Not Giving an Example

Citing four birds and explaining one of them
(this is the bird of fear of regret
and insufficient haste)
or explaining another as well (this is the bird
of it doesn't matter if there are many or few birds
gathered around me).
Not giving an example instead of explaining.

Fulfilled Desire

Running along the riverbank.
Mist on the water. A barge loaded
with bricks is going in the opposite direction.
Turning and running after the barge.

(An old woman in a raincoat
at a table. A waitress puts down a cup of coffee.
The woman stands up and walks after the waitress:
may I have a little more sugar?)

First This, Then That

   Writing, then waiting;
waiting, then writing;
   a poem, then a goodbye,
then visiting someone.

   Longing, then choosing;
exams, then waking with a start from exams;
   visiting someone,
then making him leave his house.

   He's run away frightened,
won't be coming back.
   Waiting the night in his house,
in the morning doing what I would otherwise forget.

Su Dongpo

A poem must be about something; otherwise no one can say
if the poem is superfluous if it is about him.

What he can say, what is in his heart: a poem if one is bigger than the other,
disappointed if it is not a good poem.

Someone else can forget the words that are too big or too small
like balls he has thrown in the air quickly one after the other,

but take away his poems and what does he have left?
He wants to write more poems, enough to fill half the world.

Su Dongpo, How Did Your Work Go Today?

Late in the evening, he is still sitting in his office;
must he wait until he is old to stop working?

If he can't stop working, not for a single day,
he won't know what it's like to give someone a day either.

His work is carrying out as many conversations as possible;
each day starts with a line at his door.

A man comes in, he shakes his hand,
listens to what he has to say, asks him: how did you sleep?

They would die one after the other anyway, but he has decided that they will die;
how can he give up his work and go home?

No difference between him and those who wait for him;
someone who is tired and hasn't yet eaten wants to eat soon too.

Someone else had shouted that they were free,
at least this evening and tonight.

Shotetsu on Shunzei and Teika

Teika goes to visit his father, Shunzei, after Shunzei's wife,
Teika's mother, has died.

Autumn has begun and a strong cold wind is blowing.
Shunzei looks sad and lost.

After returning to his own house Teika writes that the wind
longs for those who are no longer here.

Shunzei replies that autumn has begun, a cold wind is blowing,
and he is still weeping with grief.

Shotetsu says that he doesn't need to explain why the poem
Teika wrote is painful.

Because Shunzei is old and writing to his son, he doesn't want
to say he can't go on,

that is why he says that it is autumn and the wind is cold.
A difficult poem and a good one.

If Someone Asked Shotetsu This, This Is How He Would Answer

In which province is Mount Yoshino;
    in which province, Mount Tatsuta?

When I write about cherry blossoms, Yoshino;
    when I write about autumn leaves, Tatsuta.

That doesn't help me to remember
    that one is in the province of Ise, the other in the province of Hyuga.

But although I have never bothered to learn it by heart,
    I have discovered that Mount Yoshino is in the province of Yamato.

If my house burns down with all my poems,
    I can get some back from those who have learnt them by heart.

I won't dare to ask for the poems about who I desired.
    That's why I'll write them again when I remember who I desired.

Ryokan

This is the begging
I do every day
before returning to where I sleep.

I only have enough strength
to accept what is given to me:
as much freedom as anyone could want,

poems to read
that when I read them for the first time
made me realize I had been wasting my time.

Seen again where
I lived for a long time,
walking to and fro as if someone had left me.

As long as I am here
I can think back, think ahead,
look around me, like someone who fucks around.

Laziness and Patience

The three sons of the father who says that when he dies,
the entire inheritance will go to the laziest son.

A judge has to find out which of the sons is the laziest.

The first son says: I go quiet when I think someone loves me.

That's not bad, especially the haste, like someone
who has come to tell someone they don't love them.

The second son says: my father has worked hard his whole life
to say that the inheritance goes to the laziest son

and that it's up to a judge to find out which son
is laziest. If it was more I know what I'd do,

says the third son to the woman he spends the inheritance with
in just one night. The woman tells the judge.

The judge asks the son: how did you know that she was the woman
who would tell me about it?

Allowed to Say

Scared of no longer being able to see
those who don't know who I am
without shouting who I am.
Are you someone who is allowed to say I?

The first day I gave up the day,
the second day the night,
the third day everything except
being allowed to say I.

The fourth day my desire grew desperate.
A voice said: you are not strong enough to stay alone
with me.
I said: that's why I want it.
Heard.

John of the Cross

The most beautiful woman imaginable visits him when he is alone,
says she loves him
and that she wants him to love her.

An orchestra starts to play when he is in pain.

What does the little monk say when asked what he wants?

Suddenly he is abandoned.
He feels sick when he thinks of what has abandoned him.
Just before midnight he asks what time it is.
Please, be quiet.

Sometimes

Sometimes he is loud like Jesus;
sometimes quiet like Mary,
    with birds around him.

Sometimes he walks around like Jesus,
and sometimes he jumps up
    like Jesus's father.

When I sit down he comes to sit with me,
except when he is sleeping;
    then he stays where he is.

Poem

Writing a poem
    that is too big to fit

between what I now see and what I see
    when I am quiet.

Saying how this is,
    without saying what this is.

Trying with a poem.
    If I can't make it any bigger, it's done.

Tao Qian

If you can write you must feel love after all,
    just as: you must help govern the world after all.
Tao Qian says: I am withdrawing,
    going back to where I can better explain my choice.

    An abandoned woman's song:
someone who can help but doesn't get a chance.
    I am going back to my house
and he who waits for me because he is trapped in the house.

Choosing

The gray of the water,
    the gray of the sky
—not quite as dark, not shining quite as much—
    two fingers of a spread hand of color
to choose between: you have to look at them as if they're a wall.

Being waved goodbye.
    That was a good one.
Curious as to his successor.
    Strange being saddened.
You knew that goodbyes are everywhere.

Han Yu, Ouyang Xiu, Su Dongpo: At the End of the World

Han Yu complains when he is banished,
says Ouyang Xiu, calm when banished.

Su Dongpo worries everywhere about how to govern well,
even in a hut on the beach.

He writes what no one can write or read
from the beginning to the end

without looking around, and stands there
and looks around.

River, Mountain

After a night by a river and a mountain Su Dongpo writes:

The water poked out at me like a tongue.
The mountain like the body of someone who has left.
More explanation received than I can remember.

What I see and how I feel have nothing to do with each other.
One is not like the other, it does not contradict it.
The river is too loud, but not for how I feel.
I lie down where the river rushes past.

Dogen writes that Su Dongpo writes this
when he hears the sound of the river in the dark
and remembers what someone said to him
because it is necessary that someone pass it on.

Song

Not long ago
it rained hard,
not long ago
it got dark.

I didn't go on
until it had stopped,
so I had to wait
until it stopped.

I heard the rain
fall from great heights
and could have sat
outside on the grass.

The rain as a crown
on my head, or
as if I hadn't yet begun
and got to say when.

Like in a song:
once and once again,
afraid it has changed
or remained unchanged.

Song

The joke is
I would have liked to be with someone
who was the beginning and the end for me.

When I am old
I will say what I like about love
like a girl who's not afraid of it.

Because I thought
it wouldn't happen again
that someone could love me.

That's me, put me down somewhere
where something is about to begin
and I will start.

Is there something
I mustn't joke about here
but only outside?

But if you're with me
you don't need to laugh at it
or only after you've turned it into a song

And sung it backwards,
from the end to the beginning,
and then laugh as if in a gale.

Song

Because I had no money
I haven't slept,
I walked,
couldn't sit anywhere.

Isn't that
what I had to give back,
no less than it was,
I've hardly touched it.

What makes me hot or cold,
not because it's hot
or cold, and it doesn't
have to be enough.

Isn't that what I get,
enough to do what I like
one last time
and choose which is best.

Song

I have forgotten
what I discovered
because it is so long ago,
where do I sleep?

When I was a child
I thought I could be
between everyone
and the lights of the night.

That is what I thought,
that someone gets
what makes them shine
when they think of it.

That someone only knows
words for ever
and a day, quieter than
the day before.

Song

I read life after life
and when someone's as old as I am
I hold my breath,
sometimes I look up when that was.

When I was younger
I sometimes skipped
where someone was a child,
I don't know why.

What I want to have with me:
a book that has enough to read in it;
when I'm old I won't give it away,
I'll sell it.

I also skip
when I get scared
that someone won't change anymore,
I only read how it ends.

What I want changes
from moment to moment,
even when I've had enough
I'm sad it's over.

Michelangelo Song

Michelangelo says:
to make a thing that is like forgiveness
takes great effort and risk
of losing what one does not have.

Sensing a mistake before it happens,
but not knowing when and how large,
oh, and I forgot to say,
this is not actually what I wanted.

Michelangelo says, draw something every day,
draw something you see.
I must draw something today,
something I see.

Oh, I forgot to say,
this is not a dream,
I forgive you many things because of something
you said and have now forgotten.

You can feel love
for the first thing you see,
as long as you remember:
ending, equilibrium, measure.

Song

A day that a child
is allowed to do as it likes,
as long as it doesn't make a sound.

Lightning flashing in every room
of the house everyone
except the child has left.

The child runs into the garden
where rain lashes its face
and walks back slowly.

Over and over the sky thunders,
the child walks forward again,
refusing to be sent away.

Each time the child hears
fills it to the brim,
empties it, nothing to be done.

Even on the day the child, without
telling anyone, as allowed,
makes itself the most beloved.

Most beloved, next time
you wear out your shoes dancing,
send them to me.

Song

What it's like
to be someone else—
I've known that since I was a child
and heard a song
someone had left behind.

When I hear something said
that makes me hot or cold
I want to be that someone
and later I find out
that I am the only one who heard it said.

If I want to go
where I don't need to stay an hour,
I only need to look around
and I hear: hot, cold,
while I walk on.

If I cannot move,
because I am on the edge
of where I don't want to stay,
which I remember
because it is too much to finish.

Now the best song starts,
and I have to stand up,
like when one person starts later than the other
and whispers faster than the other
and suddenly they both say the same word together
                                          out loud.

When I Was with You Song

When I was with you
I said to you:
take off my clothes,
remove my jewels,
lay them down carefully.

To help you
I will raise a foot,
I will hold up an arm;
undress me slowly,
take off my shadow.

When I was with you
I said that to you,
while my shadow moved
left, then right,
trying to hide.

Song

Soft and heavy,
hot and cold,
thank you for
putting up with me.

What is wrong with
my wanting to have
what fills me and drains me
how should it feel?

To go from one
back to the other,
from empty and full
to what to do.

Touched by
words as well as by that
which makes a difference
between empty and full.

As if the difference
were made in me
and I, touched,
must move on.

Song

I listen to a song
I listened to
in the house I no longer have
to make them each other's.

As if depth were not needed,
dark green shrubs,
a golden bird walking past,
the days and nights part of each other.

Going Away

Sunshine on the floor, I can finish it here, don't need to take it with me.
I can't go away because they're standing in front of the house, saying: stay, stay.
I stand on the roof holding a vase and drop it so it smashes on the street.
They look at the ground, quiet for a moment, now I can go away, what else
can they say?
Was that why I was chosen, as someone who won't stay long, won't take
anything with him when he goes away?
Is it time to leave Moscow, the sun is shining, there is no snow, if this is the
Russian winter it's not too bad.
Maybe I can stay here all winter and leave in the spring when the grass is high.

In a Forest

Tell me I was left behind in a forest when I was a child, what did I think would happen when I was suddenly alone?
Was it dark when I started walking back, did it get darker and did I start walking faster?
What kind of night was it when I got back, it was a night like any other, except my meal had been eaten and someone had slept in my bed.
Does more rain fall on my head when I walk faster, when I walk faster I bend forward more, when the wind blows harder the rain falls at more of an angle.
When I am cold I have to walk faster, when I am cold I am allowed in.
It is long ago, so long ago, so much rain, such hard rain, does anyone want some ice cream, tall melting sundaes, enough to feed a bear with only rags to wear?
Now a story about three bears, one of whom did what it could; that wasn't much, shaking hands for just a moment.

What Did You Say, Don't Go Too Far Away

The chance of someone not coming back is the greatest when they haven't
been here long, that's why everyone talks to them as little as possible until
they have come back at least once.

If you have started to long for them and they don't come back, and that
happens again and again, no one else will want to talk to you.

I find it difficult to say something general without also saying something
about the sunlight when they wave me goodbye.

When someone has just arrived they have so many questions and when I don't
hear anyone else answering I say something that seems general but is about
what I once experienced myself.

As long as I stay here I can listen in case they call me back, the complete
inverse of the game children play when they have a chair too few.

They count each other out loud, pointing with a finger, starting over and over
again, always including themselves.

Looking at the moon and the stars around it, as if it's a way of getting rich quick.

Wanting to know how it ends, as if two children are playing, I walk away
before their game is finished.

The things that make me suddenly feel like I'm back and nobody's left.

At your place it's like being in a hotel, why is it strange to want to live like
that, it's what people pay for, isn't it?

If I want to hear another reason, if someone sleeps in hotels often, that's
where they know where they are in the dark.

I can also act like you're a guest at my place, please, wait until someone
comes to show you to a table, and I'm that someone, good morning, you're
saying it's almost noon?

I look at my watch and you're right, it's half past eight, you must have
overslept after a wild night, what do you mean you're too old for that?

You woke up because you thought someone was knocking on the door to your
room, but it was the door of the next room, that's how exciting your life is.

Has someone already brought you coffee or tea, otherwise I'll bring it at once,
here is the pot, I'll pour one for you and after that you can pour your own.

When you go out later, don't hesitate to ask directions from someone who
looks like me, when he tells me this evening that he was able to help
someone like you cross the road he will want to embrace me.

That's nothing to be sneezed at because he's twice my size and I am so tired by then, because in the mornings I work here and in the afternoons I'm an emissary from up in the sky.

I think that it can also be the other way round, that what reveals something can also conceal it, that's why I always want at least two tricks to do the same thing.

You say that it can also be the other way round, using what conceals to get a better view, but you're so much closer to reality than I am, you notice sooner when you say something that isn't so.

Research Report

I talk to doctors who have won the lottery: immediately after they have heard the news and then every two, three years.

The first time I ask them what they are planning to do with the money, later I ask what they have done with it.

They are almost always willing to answer, even if they have lost it all again, and the first time I talk to them I do not contradict them if they think I work for the lottery.

There are only a few who have lost it all, most of them have bought a new house and something else they had always wanted and put the rest in the bank.

Of all the doctors I talk to, there is only one whose wife left him after he had won.

It made him feel sick at heart for a few days, but once he had also spent a week longing for a woman who was dead.

At the end of that week the longing diminished, but then he realized that he had now really lost her.

Most contented are the ones who give some of it away each year: to a local hospital, for instance, to buy a new bed.

If I could do something new this late in life I would study medicine, because doctors try even harder for colleagues.

The sick doctors I talk to tell me that this is really true, and that it's a shame that I am not in any way a colleague.

Not even if I have studied everything they have studied, because if I had already done something else before, I could be a doctor and do something else on the side, or I would know what they know in a different way, because of studying it so late.

Best Not Go Blind as Long as There Is Something Left to See

We see each other growing smaller and smaller, as if we are both walking backwards, away from each other, neither wanting to be the first to no longer see the other.

No hurry as it can't go any faster anyway, making a difference after first showing what is the same.

That's what actors do, isn't it, crying at will by thinking of their dead dog?

When It Comes to My Health, Nothing Is Too Expensive, but If It Really Helped, It Would Be More Expensive

It's time for champagne, that never got anybody fat, and then to the theater.
If he can maybe stop swearing about actors who exaggerate I will be his
second tomorrow morning at all of his duels.
What does he want, to be pissed on while sitting in an empty bathtub?
Someone told him: you used to be so handsome, you could have had anyone
back then.
When Mozart was as fat as you, how long had he been dead by then?
If he can afford it—he doesn't earn more than he has—he can go live in a
house at the seaside, where the waves come up to his front door.
But first we have to visit a woman who doesn't want to let us in at first
because she's tired.
He kisses her on the cheek, she's sure to have heard that he's getting married
tomorrow, can she say something that will bring him luck?
It's the middle of the night, I stretch out on a couch when she's about to say
something, I'm too tired for this.
When she sees him walking in the street with a woman next to him she
knows it's allowed, because it's about a life, his being in good health never did
anyone any harm.
Back on the street he asks if I can lend him some money, I have to believe
him, it is not about his debts to the butcher, the tailor, the grocer.
He even tried cheating at cards to win from children, they're better off
learning what to expect sooner rather than later.
Let him choose a game nobody can cheat at or say he's stopping because he's
ahead.

Do I Have the Time Perhaps

One man speaks one language, another another, maybe I can help them agree on the price.

We're talking gold watches, I don't need to think they're beautiful.

One makes an offer, the other demands more, I translate for them until they agree at just under half the difference.

But the buyer doesn't have enough on him, he has to go back to his hotel to fetch more money, the seller can't wait because he has to catch a train.

Can I perhaps advance the shortfall, give it to the seller and wait until the buyer comes back with the money, the watches stay with me as a security.

They think they know me well enough to rely on my not leaving with the watches.

I still have one of those watches, I see that it's flicked forward an hour and turn it back, then I see that all clocks say an hour later.

I was searching for a poem by someone else, in another language, to recite—it's up to me whether I do it in that language or in translation.

That is why I wanted to find a poem I can translate myself because I don't like to let people hear how poorly I speak other languages.

What an Actor the World Has Lost in You

An actor on another actor: he turned from left to right and stopped, at the same time gesturing slightly with his hand.

Being an actor was unbearably lonely if no one noticed him doing it, the chill from its beauty went right through me.

Someone who always comes in too early or too late comes in like that, a bad actor can do it now and then, only a very good actor can do it all the time.

They are acting and they go on for too long or stop suddenly and you can see they're glad to be allowed to stop.

Is That Something I Can Learn?

Gorgias arrives in Athens as an emissary from Leontini, a city in Sicily asking for help.

This is the same Gorgias who teaches how to go from one proposition to another and how this can be used to win a court case.

The way Socrates does in an Aristophanes play, but it is Gorgias, not Socrates, who is prepared to teach anyone who will pay him how to go from one proposition to another.

One of the two generals Athens sends to Sicily is Laches, the general Socrates asks about the meaning of courage.

Afterwards they send three generals who disagree about everything: Lamachus, Nicias and Alcibiades.

First conquer Sicily, then Carthage, Italy and Spain; a good plan, but you'd need to send different generals, not Lamachus, Nicias and Alcibiades.

When Alcibiades was a young man, Socrates let him sit by his side day and night; couldn't he have taught him how to be a better general in the meantime?

That's not a problem for Socrates, but for Plato; Socrates knows how to walk home after a lost battle.

Continuing with what I do, recognizing what might be important enough to justify putting everything I have into it—both of those are brave, aren't they?

I can learn to do both, but it is difficult to learn to do the two things at once, and getting better at one doesn't make it easier to get better at the other afterwards.

If I can be brave in both ways like someone who goes from play to play, his life a succession of short trips and staying where he pays per day, can I also be brave like a general and vice versa?

Cause, Sign

A sign shows what is going to happen, a cause makes it happen.

If the sign also makes things happen there is no reason to set it apart because then I would be setting something apart simply because it is different for me.

If I didn't need to write this myself, but had secretaries I could dictate it to, I could say more about it.

If something is taken from me I think about what it would be like if the opposite were taken from me—that which causes or means what is furthest from what is caused or meant by what has been taken from me.

Someone Who Wants to Blow Their Brains Out for Love Takes It Seriously and That Is Important

I don't think I can watch you if you, the actors, can't admit it's funny.
Someone dies, but that's halfway, and someone at the end, but he kept saying he wanted to die.
Not that everyone always gets what they ask for, but nothing happens to anyone without their having asked for it at least once.
Like in a play with too many roles when I read it, but it's easy when staged.
It's even easier when all the roles are for one actor, in haste and regret that he met her so very late at night.
Please don't cry about what you have to say, otherwise I'll give you lines, you can write down one hundred times: this is so important no one can ask for it.

I Know Another One Like That

You come in, take my plate off the table, shake it off over the garbage bin, put it back down in front of me, say: I couldn't let you eat that.
Another life like this and I won't know where to start, as I heard in a dream, no longer mine, given away to the one who promised to plead my case.
You say that being with me is like remembering what you have lost forever, like when someone tells a story about someone who is sitting right in front of him and doesn't notice when he starts to cry as he listens.
Here is a plate of food, now tell a story that I know like a letter that is being held up and burnt.
It is night or morning, but it takes a long time before it gets light, the sea has reached the land, the wind comes from all directions.

In a Dream

In a dream I write a poem and just before I wake up I have already lost the first lines.

When I wake up I only have the title left, but in the dream I was already sure that I needed to find a better one.

The night before I saw in a dream how something could be better and began rewriting page after page.

I hardly read what I had written and filled all the empty space.

My children are hungry, my wife has no clothes, I fall asleep in the middle of a forest and dream about the office.

This is not my dream, this is someone else's dream, don't tell it to others before it's come true.

Before I go to sleep I am afraid of losing something, I don't know what, but in my sleep I lose everything I can see and I am not afraid.

In a dream I write a poem, in a later dream, someone asks me for a poem and I give them the poem from the first dream.

As I say this, I think I am remembering it incorrectly, in the second dream someone said that the poem from the first dream was the poem they needed and they recited it from memory.

A dream I had more than once as a child, that everything I saw stuck together and came toward me, which didn't frighten me.

My Father Says That It Is Sensible to Get into Something in Which Mediocrity Is No Disaster, Like the Field in Which I Am a Professor

He decides to obey the law, as someone who doesn't know the law but expects his children to know it, and therefore does what he can to avoid embarrassing them.

My father says that he became a mediocre man especially for me, so that no one would think I could never be as good as my father.

He would still like someone to remember him when he is no longer here, not every day, but now and then, without having planned it.

If what is left after someone's death is their part of truth, what happens to my part of untruth?

When someone is dead there is nothing left, except of my father, who walks around by himself where he is.

If I May Say So

I am running and with every step I take I get lighter, my feet are hardly touching the ground anymore.
I start to fall but it doesn't worry me.
I am lying on the ground, people look at me, touch me, and an hour later I reopen my eyes.
I can say my name and the name of someone I could stay with that night.
What I know for sure is that this is like it would be if I could say how.
This is more than a year ago, but today I go running and feel it coming closer again.
It doesn't feel right yet, but I know that if it started to feel right I would no longer be able to decide.
I know that I am where I often am, but can't say where exactly any of the things I can see are.
I go from running to walking, wobbling from left to right so as not to fall.
I sit down on the ground, my hands are shaking and my face is covered with sweat.
I don't get that many chances, that doesn't mean that if I get a chance to say no I have to say no.
Like when I say that I don't want anything else because I can't bear thinking that it's the last time.

Ghalib and One More

At court they still act like it's the old days,
  But instead of long parades with horses and elephants, the same horse keeps coming past.

It's the best they can do with what is left,
  Like the consolation of being held, the smell on the clothes.

There is enough wine to keep filling the same glass and passing it round,
  Reciting poems all night long.

I say I'm going to wash my hands, then stay away a couple of hours.
  When the night is almost over I come back and they ask me for one more poem.

After that I am the first to go outside,
  Catching sight of the woman who stands on the street till morning comes.

It is she who will receive me in paradise,
  When no one she looks at desires her any longer, she recites poems by Ghalib.

Too Much, This Much

What do you want—me to tell you I don't know much about you?
　　You're right, an eye and a throat, that's about all.

The hours I couldn't sleep, not out of longing for someone,
　　But because I was scared of what is not enough.

I am too old to join a procession, even if it's just the two of us.
　　One is the beginning and one is the end, I keep having to stop and stand still.

The bird up in the sky, what use to it are feathers, what use to it are wings,
where can it hand them in?
　　At the rose that can't bear this much evening, Ghalib lays them down next
to it, on the dark earth.

When I Hear Shouting I Can Shout Too

The dogs jump up and down and shout when someone walks past, that's
their job.
    They shout when they hear shouting, that's their job.

Shouting some more when the same person walks past again,
    Running after them if the gate is open, or is that how you lost your last job?

A dog goes from garden to garden looking for work,
    But it can't say it's ever done it before.

Go ahead and shout, no one will hear you.
    Is that what you tell yourself?

This one is good at what it does,
    It only shouts once, that's all it has to do.

Hey, There's a Difference Between the Chance After and the Chance Before. Oh, You Mean You've Done an Experiment?

If there were another world, I could do my experiments there.
    Not being able to think of a reason something would be there and not here is already enough.

In India there is a drunk man who never takes a step until he has forgotten where his previous step was going.
    How far does he get from where he started?

Unfair to whom? As soon as I am told there is something I can't do anything about,
    I want to know all about it.

If you need more time to say how to make something than to keep it,
    What do you know about it?

Ghalib wants to know things like that,
    Because he plays for money when he's in a hurry to pay off his debts.

And What Are We Going to Do Then? Can I Write That on the Wall?

I learn to write by tracing letters with my finger.
    I already know the letters but want to learn to write them again this way too.

I stand on a bed and write on the wall,
    Jumping up and down on the bed to get the first words as far up the wall as possible.

The moon in the sky like a letter from a box of letters,
    If I might not have any time left to learn to write.

When it's too dark to see the paper and I don't want to turn on a light,
    I write in ever bigger letters, spaced far apart.

Something Else

When I was a child I could have pretended I was sleeping next to someone I loved.

Perhaps later I would not have needed as many nights to learn how.

All the things I shouldn't have done when I was a child, didn't I have anything else to do then?

Every night I tried to imagine what it would be like if I loved someone, isn't that enough?

If I can say that I am so slow I always arrive late, then I have something.

If I can say that there are more examples than necessary, I can take one back.

My father said it helped to think of something I can look at for a long time,

A sailing ship on the water for instance, or whatever I can look at for a long time.

Poetry is the creation of meaning, nothing else.

Each time Ghalib thinks up a new meaning, God wants him to exchange it for something else.

A poem brings the day of deciding closer, a dream about a poem gives a day's respite.

Where words mean something, Ghalib's are law.

Desire

I wished my only problem was your not wanting to see how I desire you.
It's not a pretty sight, if I had a choice I would look away too.

Every time I stop I lay down my desire, my eyes too tired to see who is
standing before me.
Is that what I call a desire? I only want to learn how to do something.

Get changed, I mean, get undressed.
You are the only one who is left, everything around you is empty, not
because you desire someone.

Turn around, turn around, turn around.
I see you—if I say I see you, you can come out.

Ghalib complains that you are not doing your job.
What he thought was his due, if others get it why not him?

I have heard that less desire helps, but wouldn't more desire save me from this,
Like someone saving the life of someone he doesn't want to talk to?

No one knows what desire is until Ghalib says something about it.
He reads the history of the world and when he is finished, he says what is
missing.

It Would Be a Good Joke If Ghalib Was the Only Good Poet

Ghalib hasn't prayed a day in his life, should he start now he can no longer speak,
    Gesturing a number of times a day as if he would like to say a prayer?

That is Ghalib telling his friends they shouldn't stop
    Giving him their poems to improve.

Not because he loves poetry, don't be ridiculous,
    But like a woman defending the man she has been married to her whole life.

I know a secret I want to tell all my friends,
    I can tell from the poems you have sent me that they're not the first you
have ever written, and you're not asking for anything either.

Give me a poem and the next day I'll give it back improved, unless I have lost it.
    If my hands can't hold anything anymore, you mustn't give me anything
anymore.

When I am no longer here, they can give it to you, the bloodied flag I gave my
life for.
    There are many good poets but I would rather wait outside until it's Ghalib's
turn.

As Long as Possible and What Will We Say Then?

I have made my
own peace,
bypassing the others,
I said why,
is there anything else I need to do?

What has fallen from the table,
a piece of toast,
spread on the
wrong side,
now I don't need to do that anymore.

What I find difficult
is that there, in a house far away,
the difference between inside
and outside is so great
that I need so many supplies.

If I had a lot of something
I would put it in lots of places,
including those I couldn't
have thought of beforehand,
but happened to walk past.

What blew in
when I entered, how is that possible,
did I not close the door fast enough?

Perhaps I didn't see it
when I entered,
because inside was so different from outside.

The Context in Context

Avicenna reads
    Aristotle
        over and over again,
            the *Metaphysics*,
    maybe forty times.

    One day
        at a market he sees
        the brief introduction
    to the *Metaphysics*
written by Al-Farabi.

    He buys
        the book immediately
and reading it
    realizes how he should read
            Aristotle's *Metaphysics*.

    He doesn't even need
    to try it out
        because he knows that book
        by heart,
he has never been so happy.

    The next morning
he gives more money
    to the poor
        than they have ever
            had from him before.

Afterwards he walks to the market,
        is he hoping
        for another book like that
    about another book
        he has often read?

Feel free
to ask me another question like that
where all I can do
is give the kind of answer
that makes me cry.

I Love Life

What about
    being able to do something
because I still don't know very much?

      Very briefly
    being able to dance
ahead of the music, the thin shell
    of what grows faster
    than a traveler travels.

      Was I just doing something
    as if throwing something away,
or was I already trying to do something
    that is difficult,
      especially for me?

In my underpants,
    I already said that,
      like in a joke from
and for a hundred years,
for the occasion I've specially
      put on a pair that are way too big,
I told you I loved life.

    Like standing between two
      marble lions, but
this is different, this is better
    for me, and I say
something I hope is surprising
    twice in a row, what shall I
      say again now?

This is on a day
when I want to say all kinds of things three times,
    and: silence, silence, silence,
    as if it were music,
someone else's who doesn't know it.

Joke

Here's a ladder,
a broom,
and a bucket of water,
now turn it into
a joke.

The best job in the world
when they couldn't
say anything.

Now that they can say things,
here's a promise
missing three words.

The Army

You wouldn't believe

how badly this army is led,

right,

and then left again,

and then we all crawl through the mud.

So that later you can look

at the others

one after the other

and guess if your own face

is covered with mud too.

If you had enough money, you'd buy a cannon

and start your own.

Joke in a Dream

You dream you are masturbating

(you don't mean a dream that makes you come
while you are still asleep),

something you have never heard anyone else talk about

(although it would be strange if you were the only one),

that's a waste, you say.

In another dream later that night

you can no longer count
from one to ten,

they ask you:
what *can* you do?

Joke

You used to be ashamed
of letting it show
when you wanted to be moving.

Now you can
leave out
what you wanted to be moving,
leaving an empty space,
half hoping nobody notices.

You've Had Dessert and Want to Have the Same Dessert Again, Not Because You're Still Hungry, but Because It's So Good

Melt some butter in a pan,
and put the halves of an unpeeled pear
face down in it,
add a handful of sugar,
and something for depth.

Or, better still, peel a pear,
lift it up by the stalk,
lower it into a pan full of red wine,
put a lid on the pan and let it simmer
two hours at the lowest possible setting.

On the Streetcar

Your wife walked naked to the stop
and got on the streetcar,
you didn't even wave when it left,
scared they would see you still standing there,
weren't you supposed to go too?

For in the Soup or Salad, or When You Want to Decide for Others as If You Can Say, Yes, You Do Want to Be King of Persia

The prisons cancel out the prisons

and wasn't it better under the Shah after all, the successor to Darius and Xerxes,

because if you discount drunkenness, was Khomeini so different from Alexander?

Do you remember how the last Shah wanted to build a new harbor,

where there was no harbor and no railroad going there, and how were the construction materials going to get there,

and anyway, OK, a harbor, but is the sea even close to where you put your finger on the map?

You practice losing what you could say you had, like the pride and drunkenness of Darius, son of Hystaspes,

when he says yes, he does want to be king of Persia,

and later, as a reward, you can read the poem about it again, the book is open before you.

Themistocles says he can tell you, if you want to become king of Persia,

how to get each extra bit of land you also want to be king of,

and this time he really means it, it's not just a trick to get you to make a mistake.

Can You Ask Your Banker, or Another Banker Who's Still Awake, to Quickly Get Some Cheap Money, but a Great Deal, Not a Little?

If you want to rob a bank, it really is best to start with a small one because then you might remember what you wanted to say once you're inside.

That's the way to get further inside, saying you would like to talk to someone, that you have a proposition.

Or that you'd like them to explain how they can make what they keep for you grow and grow, without it blowing away in the wind.

And you can blow away as if in the wind if they follow you with an explanation, that is what you learnt when you learnt to mind your p's and q's.

They ask if you don't have half an hour to talk to a banker who's been fired. After all, you had always run out into the street right away, before they could ask you to walk to the front door with them.

Here is the box in which you can put everything that is yours, which nobody else has even the slightest right to.

You've seen that done a hundred times, or did you think that could happen to countless people instead of you?

The first day he came to work here, he immediately asked if people got fired here on Thursdays or Fridays.

Or you ask him, so you can advise him about which other job he could be suited to: if you know something nobody else knows, when do you tell it, or if somebody tells you something's urgent, how many different reasons can you think of to say, "not right now"?

ENVOI 1

Once in his whole life your grandfather was invited to have lunch with a director of what was then the Amsterdamsche Bank, later the AMRO, later still the ABN AMRO—quite an honor for a small businessman. In the course of the extended lunch, the director brought the conversation round to a particular company and related that it was an especially reliable outfit, led by a competent and very solid board. While they were waiting for coffee, your grandfather said that he wanted to wash his hands, but instead of going to the bathroom, he ran out onto the street to look for a phone booth—this was long before the invention of the cell phone. He called his office to immediately cancel all deliveries to that company and recall everything that could still be recalled. The company went bankrupt two weeks later and the Amsterdamsche Bank turned out to be not only the largest creditor but to also have all stock as collateral.

ENVOI 2
A small man,
a businessman
with his own business,
sits in the dark
with his back to a tree.

Like a Law or a Poem, for the Salafists or Constitutional Originalists, and Are We Now Suddenly Allowed to Make Jokes About What You're Afraid Of?

How long can a text that is used to determine what to do remain as if nobody's?

A proposal: that can definitely no longer continue when a decision that required understanding the text has not been made for as long as a life lasts.

You have to decide: here is the text and what you know about those who wrote it, the previous readings of the text and what you know about those who offered them, and what you know about what they knew about those who wrote the text.

Is there anything else you want to know? The customs of those who live with the text and what they know of the law, and of its readings, and of those who wrote the text and those who offered the readings, and of you who must decide.

By the way: how long may a text that is used to determine what to do remain as if nobody's?

ENVOI
Let's make a law, then we can fine those who say something strange about it. Or are we now suddenly allowed to say anything at all about a law, like about your nose?
Your nose is so long we know you are coming long before we hear your footsteps.
And if you stick your nose in your own affairs it sticks out the other side.
You have to pay as much as their face is worth if you bump into someone in the dark and you can still see it on their face a day later.
You are allowed to explain that law as you please, not like a joke that you are only allowed to explain in one single way, and the fattest angels and police officers keep watch.
Do you hear it still, and that too? Then you must have good ears, not just large ones, like your feet.

Imagine you couldn't kiss very well because your nose got in the way, and now you don't have a nose anymore.
Then you know a law you would like to start with.

What Is Yours

Aren't you the one who had so much you hadn't made yourself, scattered round you since you can remember?

The tallest girl you could find when you wanted to go back home comes home with you and when you wake up, you see that nothing is in its place anymore.

Has she also taken not having to die with her?

Why would she do that, does she have to die?

Maybe she wants to give it to someone else, she wasn't going to keep the other things she took for herself either.

There is a man at the door with a tax bill, wanting to see if there's anything here to take possession of.

The man says he's not shouting at you, he is only speaking as clearly as possible.

If he tries to lift something up you can show that it's not yours, then he can't take it with him of course.

He looks bigger than he is in all the clothes he's wearing, but that's also because it's a cold day.

Or else he comes from a state where they don't have any laws at all yet and asks if you can't give them a law or make one for them, and then it will be the only one they have.

What an opportunity, not explaining a law, but writing a new one and not one that fits between two others.

At the Races

You go to the races and don't even bet because you think *that* horse is going to win and, after thinking some more, *that* one.

They let you in because they think you bet big, but you don't have any money in your pockets and that's how you leave again too.

But if you see someone who's won big, you walk up to them and shake their hand.

Pascal writes of Montaigne that he hardly seems to worry about whether he will be able to get help later, but that isn't true.

Do you remember when you were told: you still have me to ask for help now, but not forever?

When Montaigne is traveling and sees where others lay down what they find valuable and important and leave it behind, a necklace, a ring, a hat, he does the same.

When traveling, he is less likely to want to forget how he feels about something.

Here you can place a bet on horses when there are only eight or ten or twelve racing at once and a little further along is the window for the Pascals who want to bet on everything that gives the smallest chance of what is still more than you can say.

Each of the Pascals has a piece of paper with what reminds them of the most important thing that has ever happened to them written on it.

ENVOI
What help is it if it doesn't happen to you?
That is a desire.
Learning to recognize desire, here it comes again, a storm of desire, running ahead of the wind.
You recognize that what you have been waiting for is about to happen.

Here comes what you recognize and you say you really weren't expecting it anymore.

Defending the desire for emptiness without needing to call on the reserves.

Scared of missing out on something if you don't try to fulfill a desire now while you are still capable of desire.

You want to be with someone who knows what it is to be beautiful and you not yet enough.

Are you thinking of what Plato says about the desire for beauty as a way of coming to know something?

Like what was written on a vase, next to two boys looking at each other: This is the beautiful boy.

Like what was said to a boy: Surely you haven't forgotten what you are and what happens to you?

Power and Knowledge and Justice

Imagine there is someone far away who has almost no power but loves us—
our existence matters to him and he wants to know as much as possible about
each of us.
Or else he could have power but has set the condition that he only wants to
know that much if he doesn't have to have power.
If you have had a lot of power, you can never give it back entirely, you still
know something about how it works.
Or would you rather have one who keeps his empty eye on you, not with
power over everyone, but like a secretary or a doorman who does have power
over you but not much, and you can take a lot of it away by walking off and
standing somewhere else.
You would like to be able to be polite if you get too little to show those who
have power over you, not much, how that is possible, and if they continue to
treat you like that, they don't have to do anything else for you.
Now you admit that you want power after all, at least today, meaning that you
want to use others as instruments or let yourself be used as an instrument.
Somewhere in between—or in the middle—there might be a door, like the one
between loving and letting yourself be loved, two of the directions in which
love goes.
If you lay power and love down next to each other in the middle, each in their
two directions, the doors on the left and right open to separation of bed and
board.
Those last two partly as parodies of each other, getting something into
yourself and getting into something, and practicing with something that
keeps getting larger.

ENVOI
Being right
about what can go wrong,
and not fleeing in time.

Jumping out of the window
from the third floor
when you see a mob marching into your street.

Evening

Cavafy writes about a young man
who didn't yet know what kind of career he wanted
but thought that he still had ten more years
of being handsome enough to be let in there,
where he stood outside in front of the door
in the evening.

He was a customer there,
but thought that he would still be handsome enough for that
for ten more years.

Cavafy writes somewhere else that he is moved
by a detail in the coronation of John Cantacuzenus and Irene,
daughter of Andronikos Asan.

He can say that,
just as he says that it's almost evening.

If instead of gems, colored glass
symbolizes what is appropriate to have
on the occasion of a coronation or a marriage
that is made perfect
by holding the lightest possible crowns above the heads of the bride and groom,
what is appropriate to have?

State and Market

If you are the highest representative
of the state
you walk across the market.

Where too little is being sold,
you buy what is left
before the wholesalers
make a low offer
when the day is almost over.

Or you offer loans
at an interest rate that is lower
than the banks are asking,
so the sellers can wait a day longer,
the state will earn money then too.

You start selling
what you have bought from them
when the prices have started rising
as if people are expecting
them to go up even further.

And if they themselves still have
what they can sell for those higher prices
you let them pay off their debts.

Remember, it's also your job
to keep fear
and pity apart.

In a Poem by Cavafy a Young Man from Sidon Says That
Aeschylus Gave Up Something When He Didn't Have
Anything Inscribed on His Tomb Except the Field of
Marathon Being Witness to His Bravery, and the Long-
Haired Persian Found Out About It Too——I First Read
It as the Young Man from Sidon Finding That Aeschylus
Should Have Continued to Speak as in His Plays and
Not Suddenly Like Someone in a Bar Telling How He'd
Taught a Lesson to the Man Who Thought He Was
Small and Weak, but Afterwards I See That the Young
Man Only Says That Even on His Last Day He Should
Have Thought About His Plays as Well and Not Just
About That Afternoon in the Sun, Facing the Persians

You give up something
by saying you were brave,
not just that you marched with
an army that took half a day
to pass by.

But it's not the first thing you've given up,
like on a chessboard,
and your opponent
didn't notice until the end of the day
that you'd got more in return.

Heavy, Light

You can give hundreds of examples
of what weight is, but you remember
only one.

When you weigh
one hundred and twenty kilos because
you wanted to bump into someone
who would tell you: you can't always
be this heavy.

And one more: a boy
walking between his parents
and holding their hands
while they lift him up and swing him
as they walk.

You make the light heavy,
because you're not good at it,
and don't want to learn from others.

After that you only get asked
for things that are heavy
and you hope that in the meantime
—you can't say how—
you will get better at lightness.

Yours

You remember what you wanted to be yours soon
and what you wanted in no hurry, to see
the difference.

If you remember so much, you can also be
in more of a hurry without it
frightening you.

Would you like to stand on a street corner whispering:
do you want to see a drawing
of a boy and a girl?

Because you heard that a hundred years
ago that was a good way
to make a buck.

If they remember where they come from
or something from before, they will gladly
pay more.

Look at them as if you remember them
from before, then they will try
to do the same.

What you call yours is from long before
someone said yes, like an empty street,
long ago.

Beautiful

Every night you want to watch
her stillness and her movement
until she is resting with depth and gentle splendor,
and you stop wondering if someone long ago
found her beautiful too.

And what does she say? The moon is so bright
that if you see me move for just a moment,
I won't be able to hide anymore.

You imagine what else
comes closest to that,
even remembered.

At the Start of the Evening

When you drifted ashore on a beach
a girl looked at you,
as if she were being asked a question,
not by you,
but by someone far away.

You wished her a marriage
in which she and whoever is with her
try to answer together.

You walked down the street
and walking ahead of you were two marriage
brokers.

What were they
discussing?

How badly
their last two customers
would need them.

Your Daughters

Sometimes you bump into
one of the boys in the hall after
he has just heard a no
and you can't stop yourself
from resting a hand on his shoulder
and walking with him
a few steps.

Sometimes you bump into one
in the kitchen or bathroom
who apologizes and only then realizes
he still has to introduce himself to you,
mostly they've already done that
three or four times, but they have trouble
remembering that face of yours.

More than once, one of them has said
he wants to ask you for your daughter's hand
and when you said: which one?
they got so angry
they could hit you,
although they did their best to hide it,
you saw it every time.

Those daughters of yours,
they don't even give them any hope,
even if they say yes
the whole day long. They admit to you
that they don't even know
what they're waiting for
and if you say: so you're waiting for something?
they get so sad
they would rather be somewhere else.

One of the boys asks you:
why so many? So that long before
they bring their first boy home
you can practice what to do if unexpected guests arrive
or if a single guest arrives
who lost something yesterday, or long ago,
but he can't stop thinking about it.

And maybe so many
that if you've said something to one of them
when it was still too early, you can wait longer
before saying it to the next one,
and you've already done it so often
that you no longer say any more to them
without explaining something else to them first.

You remember a man who called
olive trees, almond trees
that didn't belong to him
his daughters,
there were so many. In the evening
he took a boy who came to visit him
out for a walk among his daughters
and as it grew dark he asked the boy
if he wanted to stay for dinner and overnight,
and if he preferred to sleep outside on the ground,
under the stars,
he gave him all the pillows and blankets
he could find in his house.

A boy wants to talk with you
because he remembers something
about one of your daughters
(can you guess which one?) to do with a no
he has just heard. That is like wanting to fight
far above your weight,
but not against someone else.

The Last Thing Memory Is Best For

Being able to quote
is remembering.

De toda la memoria, sólo vale
el don preclaro de evocar los sueños.

You misremember Machado as:
the only thing dreams are good for,
and another thing dreams are good for
is being able to speak to someone
when that is no longer possible.

If you were somewhere
but not alone,
you want to be the one who remembers it,
the same when you are not the only one
who has read something.

It goes so fast,
it is difficult to read
but easy to remember.

Of all that remembering,
the only thing that is worth anything,
you misquote Machado,
who you would stand up for
if you were seated on a bus or train
and there were no seats left,
but he waves you away,
he doesn't need to sit down.

To You

What is she to you,
the girl that still belongs
to the one who left her long ago?

You still remember the dark-red earrings
on the day he gave them to her.

Your lord memory
showed you his girl,
could you say something about her
that she could say about herself
while looking at you and then back at him?

Your lord memory
is so light,
not heavy,
when he is lying on you
or beside you.

You tell
your lord memory
that you're like someone from somewhere else,
to whom he must speak
slowly and clearly.

Goodbye, Angel

An angel can tell from your face if it's the last time
you will see each other, that's why he has been called to
    look. He asks if you have something for him,
not to eat, although he's hungry, but something he can
    keep to remind him of you.

That angel only sees that whatever you are waiting for will
    no longer arrive on time. What is the worst
that can happen, that he bumps into you again after all and
    the only thing that is still yours
is what you have given him? If it's your last day he could
    give you everything he has on him,
tomorrow he will get it back again unless somebody else has
    already undressed and washed you,
although that's not necessary, as you've already washed
    yourself, like the cook who never brought food to the table
because he couldn't cook without tasting it all.

Giving a riddle as a way of asking for something: what's
    green
and lies on the ground next to nobody, a lawn. You do
    what's allowed, sitting where someone who walked away
without looking back was sitting. Giving something away
    to be allowed to do something you cautiously begin
—isn't that asking for something?

Do you remember the difference
between asking for something and asking a question,
but being asked for something is also being asked a
    question, if you still have something to give?

You wanted to be the angel
on the last day you had left, don't be afraid, you mean your
    own angel, like the cook
of your last meal, and he wouldn't have to ask anyone for

what he needed in the kitchen,
because it grew in his own garden. The madman who set
    fire to his own house has been released,
the sun is released
at dawn.

What Angels Are Good For

To find out what you have to pay attention to before you
   can start seeing what has happened to you,
not to others, or is it also possible without? First see who is
   locked up
in the distant past,
surrounded by stuff you can no longer find anywhere
because no one has kept it.

As if you had to find out
who betrayed the world, not you, in the sense of giving it
   up without getting much in return
and knowing that beforehand. Or would you just as easily
   have done the same, as if you were being asked
if you were still on the side of the angels
and you said you didn't know, but sometimes the angels still stood around you.

If you want to speak to someone you only have to say their
   name
and the angels will do their best to bring that person to you.
   They don't stare at you if you say your own name
but search for a few days and then dress an angel in clothes
   like the ones you have bought or been given
and send him to you one afternoon.

Are you on the side of the angels
or on the side of the working man? But angels work too,
don't they? Yes, but only when others have laid down
   tools. But if there's a strike,
angels can't take over the work, can they? If everyone is
   striking, no, but if it's just one person, they can.

But does an angel immediately know what to do
when he takes over someone else's work? As he didn't
   have anything else to do anyway,
he has spent long enough waiting and watching, and then

there's not many things he can't do as well
as those who have spent half their lives doing them. What
   can you do about it?

If you could say what angels are good for
you would also be able to think of a way of getting by
   without them, a description of the world without angels,
in which you yourself deliver what you have just given up.

But then you'll see too many unemployed angels on the
   street,
on park benches,
like hawkers selling what you've had for ages. And if
   you're willing to accept it anyway, they say hopefully:
you'll have to get in line!

But if you knew a way
to get all of the angels to remember from the beginning
   what they had carried from person to person
you could use that to guess a small part of what is coming.

Maybe there's an easier way
to do that,
but this would give the angels a little bit
of grace like happiness that is the opposite of the
   unhappiness of its being too cold to get undressed
while others are already naked.

Angels Bring What Can Be Sacrificed

The first angel who brought you something is still with you
    or not far away, like: is your first wife
still with you?

The angel says that you are no angel,
you can't give answers to questions put to someone else,
    even if they wanted to leave it to you.
Can you do that then? you ask the angel. Sometimes, you
    say, if you get enough clothes and makeup
to do someone else's flying test, for instance, do you still
    need to pass that test?

How do you know if someone is an angel
and hasn't simply come to stand next to you in the hope
    that you will give him something he can keep for himself
for as long as it takes to deliver? Angels don't eat and
    don't drink? They eat when they are invited
to share a meal, not alone, how will you find out that he
    doesn't do that? Try to stay with him
without his noticing. How do you know if someone is not
    an angel, touching is not enough
unless it is a giving for as long as it lasts
and the other keeps saying no, no. Would you like
    something to eat, you ask an angel. To take?
he asks in reply. He means: for himself or to take to
    someone else?

When you wanted to sit down somewhere
and walked to a field that sloped down to the east
there was someone sitting in the shade of every tree. What
    if you know what the next answer is,
but the questioner remains silent? You start to whisper
    words that did not need to be

in the question or the answer. When you have answered all
the questions you get what could be sacrificed that day,
what the sun had brought,
when it stretched that day out for as long as possible.

An Angel's Job

Angels get their jobs because they're not good at school or
    they're missing arms or legs
(the wings only help a little) or they suddenly start running
    to and fro
(they're not good at restraining themselves if they think of
    running).

Suppose there's a school for those who aren't good at
    school
and get paid to keep going to school until they've found a
    job or help
if they've already lost their parents. Would you send
    angels to that school if they'd lost their jobs
because they had to write down
what they had to do later and they have never learned how
    to do that because they had to start work right away?

Soon only angels will have jobs
because everything we do can be done differently or left
    undone. Like when you do what ensures
that the first thing they think of when they see you
is that you were once black. It's so unusual for them to need
    someone for that.

If you give something to an angel
you don't get anything in return,
an angel asks you if you know that,
as if scared that he hasn't learned how to do his job
    properly.

The angel whose wings are attached
to his skull. They tell him: it's obvious you can't fly like
    that,

but can you at least move them? He says: with my
    eyebrows, hopefully, and if that doesn't work
I can try slowly opening and closing my eyes.

That angel only pretends
to be reconciled to his great failure as that makes it easier
to accept something, even if he's been woken
in the middle of the day for it.

Stranger

What other kinds of work do you see angels doing?
   Washing somebody to look
at them one last time because it's like the work of a
   slaughterer? As you don't want to decide
when to stop looking, the light turns off when it seems like
   you've looked long enough.

There are so many things that can make someone a
   stranger,
what can you show or say to stop it? If it's so difficult, you
   can also try the opposite,
preventing them from not being made a stranger? Or would
   you rather think of an angel that prevents it
by quickly exchanging a trait as if you'd both offered one
—after all, the stranger said that they would gladly give up all
   their traits?

Or did you just dream that
when you dreamed that you were somewhere and your
   only hope was that they would make it easier for you
to travel on? The angel looks in your eyes to guess which
   trait to choose. How long does the angel
need to know you to do that well? The first time you saw
   him you thought he was a stranger.

Like when someone looks so strange that you want to warn
   a child
not to shout or laugh: if you can't help yourself otherwise,
   it's better to go outside
or, if you're outside, walk on further without looking back.

You see an angel lying by the side of the road, do you dare
   to touch him? You could pick him up with a shovel,
but isn't he too heavy for that? The wings aren't for flying,
   but because otherwise he would be too heavy to walk.

Or are you afraid they will think
you were the last to see him? If a stranger comes up to you,
do you ask them to come and eat with you? Maybe they'll
   pull a fast one on you
and you'll find your children in the soup. Do you have
   children?

The angel always does what's easiest, then you don't need
   to do it anymore,
but if there's a reward for it
you still get your share,
because an angel only counts for a tiny fraction, as little as
   he remains visible in the dark.

Revolution

Your friends who were revolutionaries
—and in the distance you see another one approaching who
    could become your friend—
live in houses that are too big for them, and faraway they
    have more houses,
where they haven't been for a long time, so you shouldn't
    think you can say something about houses
instead of something about growing old. What is it like if
    you think that only a revolution will help?

For instance, one who lives in the most beautiful house in
    Paris
and you can go there for dinner one night
and it's none of your business what is said to a stranger
    who rings the doorbell and stands at the front door
or at most you ask: surely you have someone to open the
    door? (*just* to open the door?),
but your voice stays calm,
you don't even need to do your best for that anymore. Is
    there something you want to talk about
as if the listener does not know what it is like? The wings
    of an angel are not for flying
(even if there are some who use them for that) but for
    whispering over great distances
with their shape, as can be seen from faraway, and their
    colors.

You spent many nights one after the other in a house that
    belonged to a friend of a friend
or an angel of an angel who cries out as if he wants to call
    someone back to calm him down
as it grows dark. When you were back in your own house
he came to you to say goodbye in your house to whoever
    wanted to say goodbye to him,

and it was only the next morning that you saw that he had
    only wanted
to stay one night,
but why then did he have so much luggage with him? Can
    you see anything from your house,
the ocean? A park with oars standing upright,
a fish with its mouth
full of hooks,
just look how many wanted to have me. What remains of
    you when every fish or angel has traveled a day
away from you. You move your nights forward, then
    backwards.

Is it going to start again with fury about the redistribution,
    and only afterwards
about the distribution? You want an uprising in the streets?
That works better if the fans of the soccer clubs join in,
the Galatasaray and Fenerbahce supporters in Istanbul, like
    once the Blues and the Greens
in the Hippodrome in Constantinople. You don't think you
    will be able to
predict the outcome five minutes sooner
by recognizing that at most it provides an opportunity to
    be able to explain it
once you've stopped watching.

Your friends who are suddenly poor
after they have given you what you asked for, no longer
    able to live in their big houses,
but in houses as small as when they were children. What is
    an uprising that's not a revolution? Heaven is where the
        angels are or what the angels rebel against
when they get scared that it can only postpone its downfall,
not prevent it. If an angel gets old he becomes just like you
    (as in: surrender those wings),
but for a long time he looks much younger than he is,
as in: have you ever thought of becoming a model, you are

too old for walking back and forth
where everyone can see you, but your face could hang above
   the bottles of perfume
   in shops at airports, three times life-size. Because I look
like I no longer have any wings?

End of the Season

It keeps getting dark earlier, but that too must end and turn,
continuing in another direction,
tilted back toward the sun that erases all results. Saddened
    at what passes
and you can't do anything about it (as if you want to know
    for sure, though that would make it deeper,

so you won't regret it later). Like counting the days until
    you can go back,
and if it's two days
you think, tomorrow is my last whole day here. Like
    tomorrow being the last day
I will see the sea this summer. Like quickly doing
    something

because it could be the last time. Your schedule on the
    wall, the games
you've already lost crossed off
like a prisoner's days. Maybe a new season has long since
    started,
but they haven't told you, scared as they were

that you would start running with your eyes shut. Those
    who want to can start the season later
with a game that hardly makes any difference, the winner
    gets a cup and those watching
don't dare ask,
what was that for? You might just as well ask what the
    seasons are about.

No Farewell Game

Is that even a thing? Breakfast you can also eat
when you come back at the end of the night. Maybe there's
     a field
close to where you want to sleep, and they're just standing
     there
because they haven't got a ball yet. An evening in early
     autumn, with a full moon

at the end of the field,
at your back in the second half. Did you let yourself be
     promised before the game started
that you would at least get a second half? Which you save
for when you have trouble falling asleep, and for later,
     when you have five minutes

and don't want to sleep. Is it only when you don't need it
     for one that you use it
for the other? Not a farewell game, because they don't
     usually make any difference
—and if they do,
it gets torn apart by the farewell and everything else. You
     can get sad

about the everyday continuing. Not like someone who, every
     time they hear someone else
say they find something beautiful,
answers, almost on behalf of what's being found beautiful:
if you'd like it, it's yours.

Away Game

Before you'd even seen a game
and were joining in for the first time,
you ran, not fast enough to get there on time,
but in the right direction. They thought they'd found
   a child prodigy,

but you were older than you looked. The others had
   worked for years
before first taking to the field
as if they were being paid for it too. One of them had been
   a soldier in an army
on a day they lost their way

in the mountains. Did you think someone like that would
   be scared of arriving late for an away game,
a half day's travel away,
to run around on a field there until he's out of breath? If the
   bus had already gone
he would start walking, maybe someone driving past
   would give him a lift

and he'd arrive before you. You are the only one who's
   never done any other work
and if you weren't on time to travel with the others
you wouldn't dare say on your own
that you had to go in that direction too.

One Day

One day when it's raining,
so hard you ask yourself: your last day here,
will it be like this too? The ball doesn't bounce, it floats
    away in the water. It's raining hard,
the game has to be called off. That little bit of rain?
    It's raining so hard parts of the field

are underwater. That little bit of water? It's your farewell
    game,
what good will it do you
if it gets canceled? That little game. As if what can only
    be said about you
will be erased,

as if you're already taking a shower, not in the locker
    room
but in your own house. That little bit of water. And that
    is the last game
in which you were planning to score a goal from so far away
that another player wanted to act like he's shining
    your shoe. It's raining so hard,

it's about to get dark,
you won't be able to dry out in the sun. That little bit
    of sun, not even a newborn animal
could dry out in that. What kind of animal? A mouse,
a little monkey, not much of an animal.

Farewell Game

As if you had never played before,
you wanted the winner of your farewell game
to immediately be champion of the world. It has to be full,
    the air loud with singing,
and what else do you need to make it like a necklace for
    just one neck? Think of when you wanted

the whole world to have one neck,
one throat, just for stroking. Do you let those who
    only came to watch play too,
if only for a moment? Birds are circling in the sky
over the field. How do you see those who think they only
    need to make the players on the other side

scared they're going to lose
and if there's nobody else on the field
they scare the birds in the sky? And by scared you
    only mean that you are close to something
you don't know if you can touch and live. Champagne in
    almost invisible glasses

you can take home after you've drained them. A magnificent
    sky over the field,
with a motionless rainbow
and clouds closing in fast,
like a night that might be over at any moment.

Is This What a Shallow Loss Is?

You wanted your last game to be something like a victory
    too for the others,
but inasmuch as it was,
it wasn't one that made it easier
to never take to the field again. When you're about to tell
    the others that you've won,

you think about what you shouldn't see
if that were true. You find it difficult to watch someone
    who is playing their farewell game
and also loses,
but not if it's your own game, losing always made too little
    difference to you,

not because you were so calm and brave,
the most trivial things make you scared and angry enough
    when you don't want to watch. Sometimes
when you don't want to watch something, your eyes close
    for a moment
because they want to spare your heart, which is already
    torn to make it easier next time,

like when you don't want to see someone naked,
    because you're scared
that you won't want to see others naked afterwards either.
    How to make a lost game
something like a victory too; yes, that's what you'd like to
    know,
proud as you are of how fiercely, and then no longer, you want
    to know something.

Alone with You

You wished you could say one thing
because the other had been said to you
as to someone standing on a field: you don't know what
    it's like when thousands whisper your name
because they're scared of startling you, and you hadn't yet
    made a mistake,

it could be your farewell game,
and you say you know that. To be alone with someone,
    as for a farewell,
visiting every day and being welcomed like you're
    someone else. If you only consider that,
you'd say you've had a lousy life, but that's not the case,

it was something others only dream of. Every night crying
    about who you want, about yourself as well,
it's not as if you could do anything about it, you wanted to
    be the last one
to say this. Are you going to start hoping you will still do
    something that will make them ask
if you want to join in next time too? You've already said
    goodbye

but stand there as if you can do it over again. If I say
    goodbye too soon, you say,
put me down upside-down. Or else you've walked on
to where you think
you'll be out of sight. It's my pleasure to tell you the night
    will be long.

When the Messiah Comes

When the Messiah comes
someone will have to convince him he's the Messiah
and that someone can't be a Jew,
because Jews who hear that the Messiah has come

have to carry on
with whatever they're doing. Would it change the world
if everywhere in the world
there had been at least one Jew?

(I'm not really much of a traveler.) Traveling to a place
I have never been before
is like starting the world all over again,
but I am not a good traveler. If so many have already come

and every day is filled with newcomers,
I can't be the only one
who is not a Messiah (and my not being good at traveling
is a sign).

One or Less

Tell me as precisely as possible what you want to hunt,
then I might be able to help
you search, even if it doesn't
exist yet.

As if you still remember and I have promised you
that I can travel through time
to tell you
where it is.

I remember selling fake fur
made by a manufacturer who thought up the fur first
and only then the name
of the animal.

I can imagine someone wanting to shoot
precisely that animal, with one bullet
or less, just as a Jew believes in one world
or less.

The Sabbath of Consolation That Follows the Destruction of the Temple, the Place of Which I Could Say: If You Want to Seek Me at the Beginning of the Evening I Will Be in That Place That Is Easily Found

If there is something I have to do every day,
there is a day of the week I don't need to.

That is all the Sabbath means,
and I am allowed to think that on the Sabbath too.

I can declare the Sabbath every day,
heaven and earth were made that way too.

As if I have to make something new every day,
and on the Sabbath I make what already exists.

There Goes the Spinozist

Being a Spinozist for a day or so,
but only where they've never seen one before.
It's only when they see what I'm doing,
seemingly for no reason, that they ask: do you just do that
because of who you are? There goes the Spinozist,
the children on the street shout, as if they alone recognize
who is following the etiquette of a long-dissolved court
as to how to stand, how to greet others,
how to walk on.

Look, there goes another one
on the way to the Spinozist, to take off his shoes
and sit on the floor
a few meters away from him
until the Spinozist asks if his colleagues have once again
decided to keep their distance.

Don't try something out to see what it's like,
but see how it changes or can change
the sense of freedom of someone who has consented
to being sent away for a while from all the rest: not pleasure
and seeing someone or something as its cause,
but how pleasure changes
and also the cause, and the relationship between those two,
and how much I still assume
this to be the strongest relationship between them.

Another way Spinoza was right about at least something:
when love is what shines a light on the other
among those who are like them (why them,
simply because they walked down the street one morning?)
one cannot be loved back
by who or what never has enough time
to explain it.

There goes the Spinozist,
polite to those he sees sometimes in the morning,
sometimes at night,
as if it's his last day here before traveling back
to where he can be alone for longer
and when a list is made of his possessions
and debts (as if for someone who has not seen him for so
     long
and may yet decide to refuse the inheritance)
it is so long because he always took one share
of everything he could participate in.

More Than Twenty-Five Years Too Late

More than twenty-five years too late
I watch episodes of *Seinfeld* and even *Friends*. Back then
I couldn't bear even a minute. Because it was too familiar,
too close? And yes, when I was in New York with a girlfriend
she wanted to go into the diner from *Seinfeld* and I refused,
and another time with another one I saw it across the road
but didn't mention it. Now that I've seen episodes of both,
I say: how realistic, not just the clothes
but talking and moving like in a rehearsal—not yet
a performance with an audience, if it ever comes to that—
of a play (and all acted),
but I wasn't often there or only on the verge
of being falling-down drunk, though I did have to sit down
on the floor two or three times,
and I always knew what I had said and done,
if not always who to. Writing my telephone number
in the dust on the table, in the mist on the window,
and don't look down when you call me. Who can be
the most childish, won by the one who wins
—because maybe everyone wins—and stays childish,
and what do they win? Those who are left
get to say. Jerry Seinfeld also looked too much
like Joost Zwagerman (who I scarcely knew and almost
never spoke to), not that he really looked like him
except in the proportions of the legs in the pants
and the hair on the head,
and Rogi Wieg (who I scarcely knew, but it seemed a lot)
looked like Jennifer Aniston. Something else
in *Seinfeld* and *Friends*: all the answering machines
(I just came in and heard you leaving a message)
—starting from the late eighties I could use cassettes
(the same ones as for music) I rewound when full
until the tape broke and I threw them away
(and that's another reason I can't listen
to twenty-five-year-old messages). Just change one digit

in a telephone number so you can say
later that it was by accident, or two to be on the safe side,
or all of them, as long as it still looks like a telephone number.

I can now watch the comedies from when I was young
for half a day. Back then it was still too close
and that's not bragging
or playing myself down. And if I attach *Friends*
to one side of Rogi, what goes on the other? I too can say:
I was almost an anti-Nazi, why should I apologize for the fact
that Celan's pathetic delivery—also described as too Jewish
and like something from the days before close-ups—
reminds me of Josef Goebbels (in the speech when he asks
what they want)? The shame when Celan comes close
(only too close?)—not as a Jew, but as a poet,
worse still, as a good poet, with Rilke trying to hide
behind him (autumn in a Paris where everyone is Jewish
or can become it painlessly, like Ruth in a field at dusk),
but I can always trade him in (which I do immediately)
for the Mandelstam who lives in two apartments
in the same building, on the same hall with Pasternak,
Akhmatova, and Tsvetaeva, I began to feel something
for someone, maybe you can guess who
—if something like that is said, recited,
I can't stay quiet, otherwise I'm just as much
to blame, the walls here are as thin as paper
being written on from both sides.

In the Name Of

In the name of Maimonides, Meister Eckhart says
that saying something about he who is
only takes one further away (and I say:
further from that saying)
and if he is not in any way comparable to anything else,
saying he is is no better than saying
he is not. And Meister Eckhart says, almost,
not even almost in the name of Yeshayahu Leibowitz,
that asking something from he who is not,
unless for himself,
is idolatry.

And in the name of Meister Eckhart, I say
that people can start worshipping their keeping of the law,
and in the name of Yeshayahu Leibowitz, I say
that they can just as well do that
with the intention of going beyond that worshipping,
and if they do, their worshipping of the law
takes them just that little bit further away from idolatry,
simply because it is the easiest way of not keeping it,
from which I conclude that acting like the law does not exist
to make it even easier takes them so far away
that they no longer need to be banished.

In the name of Rabia Basri (Rabia means the fourth,
as in the Hebrew *arba*, because she was the fourth daughter,
like the fourth of four sons
who by remaining silent asks his father
which of them he will tell first that the Jews live in the world,
not somewhere else), Yeshayahu Leibowitz, with
a burning torch in one hand and a bucket of water in the other,
could have gone to the place where he who is not is
and if that place had come to meet him halfway,
he could have said: if the lord of the house is not at home,
I don't need to see the house either.

And that is what I say when, instead of concluding
from the world who is not, I do it from who I can encounter
walking in the garden at the start of the evening
in a gentle breeze
and from how much retraining a Jew like me,
famed for his lawn-mowing, needed to lay out that garden
and maintain it (like a divorced woman
in the style she is accustomed to).

Yeshayahu Leibowitz says in the name of Maimonides
that the law is so generous as to allow Jews to keep the law
in the hope that he who is not will try a little to be,
just briefly, simply to do them a favor,
perhaps the day will come when they are only Jews
if they only do it because it is the law,
even if they are already better Jews
if they only do it to cross
he who is not. I say: Jews who don't keep the law
only to be able to say it didn't fall in their lap,
may as Jews (what are those Jews not allowed as Jews?)
strip those they see serving idols (as if to serve
what they don't offer their other guests)
of their Jewishness. In their own names they say
that one cannot conclude from "he made heaven and earth"
that he who did that can give away part of the earth
to whoever he likes, but heaven and earth were made
so that people can think
that they are the first to think that heaven and earth
were made for them.

Interpretation Rule

If the same story
is told twice I have to read the second
as enrichment and development
of the first, Rashi writes. One of the interpretation rules,
like laws of nature,
he finds by going on with his reading, which is the same
as translating and translating back.

Rashi finds the same-story-twice rule
right at the beginning. How to read it if I expect
a story to be told twice
and it isn't? Like when I am hoping for one more question
to help me find an answer
to an earlier question. Or is that something
I mustn't tell others, no matter how often I hear it?

But what is it like when I want to say I don't need to know
how this ends? Enough stories,
all I want now is interpretation, because I see them
diminishing before my eyes,
but interpretation lasts.

When to use someone else's line
or story without saying,
when to interpret a text that has been translated so often
it only just gets through?

My Nation Lives

When my father was in the bathtub with the newspapers
and the radio, he would half rise out of the water
after hearing the news on the hour to tune to another station
that had news on the half hour (I could ask him
if he thought the world had changed a lot in half an hour
and he'd shrug: if you've grown old enough,
you have a right to thoughts you know yourself
to not be entirely reasonable).

I don't know if my father ever read a single poem
by Yehuda Amichai (the only poet I've said
"I just wanted to shake your hand" to), but he read
as many Israeli writers as possible
(who knows how long there will still be Israeli writers?)
and how could someone who wrote later in life
that he was no longer sure whether he could call himself
a Socialist or a Zionist not want to read what was written
by someone who chose the name My-nation-lives
because it sounded "Socialist, Zionist and optimistic"?

After my father had appointed himself
assistant general of the dispersion,
he drew a new strategy on folded-out maps:
marching into history, instead of advancing fast enough
to emerge from it. It was just one of his many strategies,
like an Odysseus alone in his wooden horse,
as in a bathtub with the newspapers.

There is a poem by Yehuda Amichai about telling his father
that he "had gone to another synagogue,"
when that wasn't the case. With my father I went to six
or seven different synagogues on the Day of Atonement,
like visiting the Parthenon, Notre-Dame, and the Alhambra
in a single day.

A novel, a painting, a ruin on a hill
is also the conversation about it,
even when there's no one to talk to. For my colorblind
and tone-deaf father
that conversation was almost everything,
often everything,
and that made the emotion he felt not only no less honest,
but also no less deep.

World, Are You Still There?

I didn't hear
from you for a while and that's why
I wanted to get in touch, please excuse me
if I've woken you
or interrupted you
while you were slipping off quietly. World, are you still there,
I say, as if someone could take me
for a Messiah. The Messiah, is he a Jew? Probably not,
because Jews don't like to do something
when someone else who isn't there, and not just a little,
but in all kinds of ways,
wants to take the credit. More reason to assume
someone is the Messiah
when he arrives
like someone politely leaving
at the earliest possible moment.

Strange

A Jew is someone who,
when doing something as strange as praying
(something you race through as fast as possible
so you're ready to start talking
while the others are still at it),
prays to a stranger,
who is like a stranger in the storm
and in righteousness and in pity,
says the Jew,
and as I hope I will remain a stranger
surrounded by my own strangeness (in the sense
that it is different,
maybe just that it lasts longer
than I expected) and if someone says
that's asking for something I will not contradict them,
because that would be ungrateful of a stranger.

I say: strangeness has taken possession of me,
I have strange thoughts,
they are the only ones I still have.

What Poetry's Good For

If asked what poetry's good for,
I always make it slightly bigger than defensible,
that's the agreement among poets who understand
their trade a little. For the second time this week I've read
an attack on Brodsky for saying that writing poetry
is the highest goal of the human species,
an accelerator of consciousness
and of comprehending the universe—and now I want to say
he's right, not just because that's the agreement,
and despite not always finding his poems
very forceful. This is Brodsky who was asked by a judge
what his job was and when he said he was a poet,
the judge asked who had appointed him (the best story ever
about a judge and a poet), and this is Brodsky who tried to be
two or three poets (why so few?), and the only time
I met him was with two or three other poets in a restaurant,
where he drank quickly and started singing in Russian,
as if he were five or six boys and girls
who had come to do an audition
to be appointed as him. And then comes the day I give up
and make my way to Artaxerxes who offers me what I accept,
but it's not what I wanted. What I can say about Themistocles
comes from a poem that is so intense I don't need to know
the exact words. The one who said of Cavafy
that he could be better still in translation
didn't even know the language
the poem was written in. Brodsky was allowed to say it
because he knew the price of exile,
as Herbert wrote in another poem. The "well done" from those
of whom I used to think, when I was young,
that we might as well
give them what they wanted. Brodsky also said of Cavafy
that he only used the vehicles of his metaphors,
the reader can choose whether to look back
to see what the metaphors are for

—I think I know what he means, but I'm not sure
the word metaphor is the most correct. The only time
I met Brodsky was when I was invited to Poetry International
for the first time for the whole week of the festival,
and halfway through the opening-night poets' dinner,
I walked out and continued on to the train station
and only returned to Rotterdam three days later,
on the day I was scheduled to read (the night I met Brodsky),
because they had called me in an angry panic
while I was standing in the sun
on my balcony. Which doesn't mean I have to admit
that what someone doesn't understand in a poem
is a greater understanding,
although I can keep quiet if that helps
someone through the pain, or else I say: let's talk again
when you're feeling better.

When the Others Are Far Away

One day I hear that a non-Dutch poet is dead
and I already heard it a few days ago
but hadn't given it any more thought, which is different
from forgetting it, and it was the one
who had sailed as the only passenger on a freighter
from one French-speaking island to another
across the Atlantic and then the Pacific
—and he had only learned French later in life,
not as a small child— to make an anthology
of the poetry of those islands for a publisher who paid
all of his traveling expenses. There are Dutch poets
who remind me of each other
because one worked on a ship for two years,
the other drowned while a passenger on a ship

(a ship's doctor asks: a sharp or a dull pain?)

and who would I like to tell me "stay young forever"
or "a polar bear kills a Dutch poet"? When the Dutch poets
are all together in a boat
that was hung up on the deck of a ship and trying to row
through the ice floes to a more southerly latitude

(if a polar bear is sleeping on one on its back
—like a bearskin in front of a fireplace but upside-down —
is that a good sign?)

and we say: "a tropical night" if the daytime temperature
was above however many degrees and in the night
it doesn't fall below however many less, to bring it closer
to what they call nights in the tropics,
like transferring a balance. I have reconciled myself,
as if to the gentlest of all fates, to being en route
to addressing the poetry of the whole world

from a balcony on an empty square,
as if that could be one touch in a series of touches,
as if they would never end.

E Agora, José

Wanting to return to the Netherlands,
because of poems about the Netherlands as a well-known place,
and their poet was willing to go so far for poetry,
"he set out to see the Netherlands,"
but the Netherlands no longer exists,
not even in the dark, just as utopia is where a well-known place
was supposed to be, just as utopia is the place
that has to be well known. Those I might be addressing
don't know how to answer yes or no to that
and how could they, like when I arrive at a beach
and say that if I don't hear a convincing counterargument
everything that lies beyond will be joined to
where I come from. (Like the man in Faverey's
morning-of-the-longest-day dazzling "Gorter at the Seaside,"
serving tennis balls at the sea and going to collect them
when he runs out, including the few the sea
has laid back on the beach, like a dog letting a tennis ball
roll out of its mouth.) We don't have any colonies anymore,
José, and I don't know
the Dutch for *going native*. I can't see the sea
from where I'm standing,
not even in the dark,
I think I'm being told: "I still have water
I can pour out over you,
but what then?" I'd rather give up,
but how do I say that
if I don't want to say no? And saying "What now, no?"
like
"What now, José"? That is not the poem,
but I like to name
my poems
after other
poet's.

Lex Julia Repetundarum

I can serve as a representative of a colony
seeking recompense from a poet who has enriched himself
at the cost of that colony,
that is according to the Lex Julia Repetundarum
(if not a word of mine has been read, can I write
as if I had written the poems of the writers I have heard of?).
Can this be used as a defense against Dutch poetry
having made so little use of the poetry
in the then Dutch colonies,
and against Dutch poetry's not wanting
to make itself more useful to those who would still like
to make the Netherlands a colony? What is the point of a colony
if there's no one there who wants to recite
my poems the moment I look up
from the paper? I have after all studied history to construct
almost analogous models (history-writing, mathematics,

the two invented methods and historyless poetry between them,

not or hardly invented). There are poets who make me think,
"a civilian," when civilians are what soldiers are not,
as if I were in an army (for someone who
has always kept his distance from armies and wars,
I have appropriated a lot from them). I have heard about soldiers
taking books of poetry to the front,
but not about Dutch soldiers and Dutch poets,
perhaps because we only floated through the sky there,
dropping what we didn't want to take home with us
as if it were slipping through our fingers.

(How can Dutch poetry
help decolonization—first send a ship
full of Dutch poets who don't know how to walk in the jungle,

then send a ship to pick up those who manage
to make it back to the sea, and the spare bunks
are for civilians who have been promised something
by having them learn Dutch?)

Question: So Are Poets Not Allowed to Be Bad at Their Trade? (Answer: If They're Poets, They Can Be as Bad as They Like)

Question: why haven't they
ever asked you for that? and answer: because they thought
I wouldn't be very good at it. As if the question were:
write a short dialogue, two or three sentences,
that ends with: "And what did you think they thought
you wouldn't be good at?"

(Is this for an exam or for a sample sentence
to explain something that can always be taken
one step further back?) Finish the sentence
"All of Dutch poetry is a metaphor for..."

like something that only brings what can be loaded and unloaded,

not the wheelbarrow itself,

pushed across the border (always one step further back),
by the company Transporter, Transporter and Transporter,
of whom the second also went by the name
"Viceroy of the Underworld," because a metaphor
does not only allow a conclusion to be made,
or is one itself,
but is also a way of increasing confidence in a conclusion
when only its beginning or end is visible,

like a box that someone carries on a cord around their neck
and also holds in their hands,
with a handle to blow up something far away. I am one
of the ones they spent a long time
reworking, polishing, until they saw they had gone too far
and carried me away in the dark
after which they had long stopped expecting

to see me here again (if this is like hearing "he is no more"
they can carry me away). It was easy for Michelangelo
to get a metaphor for making something
by finding it in a block of stone,
how can writing a poem be like that?

Dream of the Beginning and End of Dutch Poetry

Other poetry was written by I don't know who,

the Dutch by the Dutch poets themselves,
who built dikes between what could be spoken of as a dream
and what could not,
behind which nobody wanted to live anymore,
the last ones leaving after the last flood
—why live by the sea when you can't see it anymore,
just a wall? Further away in the sea the bodies of poets lie

like breakwaters that let the water wash over them

to rob it of some of its power. Everything tested
a thousand times in the wave pool where name clouds
are nailed to the ceiling
(yes, like pinned butterflies). In which positions
can I still fall asleep
before Dutch poetry is over? I do the same thing I do
in the daytime in so many of my dreams
that I am so glad when it's something completely different
for once, something I can't manage in the daytime,
that for a long time
I don't want to talk about it. My not being able to say
how it began is an indication
it could be a dream. Dutch poetry starts with searching
for where one dream ends
and the next begins, like someone saying "where I end
and you begin," because I can't defend
the transition very well. A dreamed person selling dreams downstream

knows that if a good prize is named after him
no one will say no (and the whole of the Netherlands
is downstream,
behind it only sea).

If I Want to Know What Poetry's Good for,
It's a Question I Must Also Allow

Poets write less than the day is long,
even if they write as much as me,
and even less when they remember, because night is falling,
how they lost everything, except the few words
they found again. In the army of poets I wait,
like the others, for what sounds like it was once orders,
and how would I have it formulated? I write to be translated,
because this language of mine is the language of translations,
and a translator, any translator,
is allowed to break poems open, combining them,
like Fitzgerald with Omar,
if they think they know me well enough
to drop a pebble in a cup
because morning has come: dear poets, it is time
for what you say every morning,
meaning: for the rising. When would poetry
no longer be of any use?

In an army born of a self-declared necessity
I practice how much I can bring together
and I am not even the only one in that army
or the last to come in—every now and then I see a new recruit,
carrying his breakfast somewhere on a plate,
waiting to be noticed and received by the others—
as if they would look up from what they are writing at the tables
where they are seated
at the one who has appeared before them.

Poetry does not do much,
but compared to what? Poetry does not make the dead rise,
lie down again, rise again,
but sometimes it makes the rising rise. Do I already know
a way of carrying on

writing poems when I am no longer as good at remembering
     what I read yesterday that made me rise to my feet
before I noticed what I was doing? When it gets quiet
and I look at a clock (someone's watch,
on their wrist) and remember: this is the hour
when what I've forgotten
the beginning of ends. How much else do I need to know
to write poetry? At most as much as the salt
you hold between thumb and index finger or the salt
that is already in the food,
and the cook doesn't need to cry over the pots.

It is already in being moved or feeling compassion
or in everything
not going away at once. But when I said something
because I knew something,
I wanted it to be poetry and nothing else.

Wanting to become a poet
who has "translators" (I would never call myself a translator
without quotation marks,
except perhaps from yesterday to today
and to decide which parts to leave
where they are) who cannot read
the language *from*. (Making a new language
from found words and only as a bridge language
to translate poems into and out of into a third language
and to worry that Dutch is already that language,
or do the best found words have to be lost first,
like the names of those who are no longer coming?)

The poems the others left behind
when I yelled them forward, it's already enough
if I can pick them up and read a line
to get one of them moving again, now in a different direction,
like a scout who has come back frightened,
or if a line from one of their poems echoes in my head

when I say something that sounds like it,
and if it's not enough, sounds like it in combination
with a line from a poem by someone else again,
and a line from a poem by yet another
that was only just translated
before the language lost its last speaker,
from three I make one, if I can't manage with two,
or from a larger number, counting back as far as I can,
and I know it goes further.

My scouts, the vanguard, the part of my army
I still think I will be able to manage without right at the end,
including the poets from not far away,
who were still here not long ago,
but what do I do if what they left behind too soon says
what they and I might be planning. I can't follow
every one of them to pick up all the paper,
but I can send them forward so quickly
that nothing we might be planning can be carried out
exactly as written down,
and that will have to be enough,
after all, I am the kind of poet who doesn't worry about a few
extra dead on my side.

TRANSLATOR'S ACKNOWLEDGMENTS

THE FOLLOWING TRANSLATIONS were previously published, sometimes in slightly different versions, in the collections *Advance Payment* (London: Anvil Press Poetry, 2013), *Divan of Ghalib* (Buffalo: White Pine Press, 2016), and *Of Great Importance* (Santa Barbara, CA: Punctum Books, 2018).

"First This, Then That," "Su Dongpo," "Shotetsu on Shunzei and Teika," "If Someone Asked Shotetsu This, This Is How He Would Answer," "Song," "Song," "Michelangelo Song," "What Did You Say, Don't Go Too Far Away," "Research Report," "What an Actor the World Has Lost in You," "Is That Something I Can Learn?," "Someone Who Wants to Blow Their Brains Out for Love Takes It Seriously and That Is Important," and "My Father Says That It Is Sensible to Get into Something in Which Mediocrity Is No Disaster, Like the Field in Which I Am a Professor" are from *Advance Payment*.

All poems included in the section "from *Divan of Ghalib*" were first published in the book of that name.

"For in the Soup or Salad, or When You Want to Decide for Others as If You Can Say, Yes, You Do Want to Be King of Persia," "Evening," "State and Market," and "In a Poem by Cavafy..." are from *Of Great Importance*.

"Heavy, Light," "At the Start of the Evening," "The Last Thing Memory Is Best For," "What Angels Are Good For," and "Revolution" were first published on Poetry International Web.

SZILÁRD BORBÉLY In a Bucolic Land
Translated by Ottilie Mulzet

NAJWAN DARWISH Exhausted on the Cross
Translated by Kareem James Abu-Zeid; Foreword by Raúl Zurita

GLORIA GERVITZ Migrations: Poem, 1976–2020
Translated by Mark Schafer

PERE GIMFERRER *Translated by Adrian Nathan West*

W. S. GRAHAM *Selected by Michael Hofmann*

SAKUTARŌ HAGIWARA Cat Town
Translated by Hiroaki Sato

MICHAEL HELLER Telescope: Selected Poems

RICHARD HOWARD RH ♥ HJ and Other American Writers
Introduction by Timothy Donnelly

LI SHANGYIN *Edited and translated by Chloe Garcia Roberts*

CLAIRE MALROUX Daybreak: New and Selected Poems
Translated by Marilyn Hacker

ARVIND KRISHNA MEHROTRA *Selected by Vidyan Ravinthiran;*
Introduction by Amit Chaudhuri

MELISSA MONROE Medusa Beach and Other Poems

VIVEK NARAYANAN After

SILVINA OCAMPO *Selected and translated by Jason Weiss*

ELISE PARTRIDGE The If Borderlands: Collected Poems

J. H. PRYNNE The White Stones
Introduction by Peter Gizzi

ALICE PAALEN RAHON Shapeshifter
Translated and with an introduction by Mary Ann Caws

JACK SPICER After Lorca
Preface by Peter Gizzi

ALEXANDER VVEDENSKY An Invitation for Me to Think
Translated by Eugene Ostashevsky and Matvei Yankelevich